New Mexico

OFF THE
BEATEN
PATH™

TODD STAATS

A Voyager Book

The
Globe
Pequot
Press

Old Saybrook, Connecticut

Cover map © DeLorme Mapping

Library of Congress Cataloging-in-Publication Data

Staats, Todd
    New Mexico: off the beaten path / by Todd Staats — 1st ed.
        p.   cm.
    "A Voyager book."
    Includes index.
    ISBN 0-87106-243-7 : $9.95
    1. New Mexico—Description and travel—1981- —Guidebooks.
    I. Title.
    F794.3.S73   1991
    917.8904'53—dc20   91-21101
                                                                CIP

Text illustrations by Carole Drong

Manufactured in the United States of America
First Edition/Third Printing

For my parents and Shawna,
and for Catherine

Acknowledgments

Though I couldn't incorporate all their suggestions, this book benefited from the input of several members of the Tourism Association of New Mexico (TANM) as well as those of the Old West Country organization. In addition, many of the state's chambers of commerce, convention and visitor bureaus, and the New Mexico Department of Economic Development and Tourism (including its *New Mexico Magazine,* an invaluable research tool) provided key leads. Thanks also go to Renée James. I'd like specifically to thank Jo Kaestner for her keen eye and deep knowledge of New Mexico's special spots. But mostly I'd like to thank Catherine for providing continual support and patience during this project and for giving up months of weekends to go "on the road" in The Land of Enchantment.

About the Author

Todd Staats is a New Mexico–based free-lance writer. He is a previous staff writer and managing editor of the *New Mexico Business Journal* as well as a former managing editor of *Albuquerque Monthly* and *New Mexico Monthly* magazines. In addition to his writing, Todd is the communications director for a statewide trade association.

Todd lives in Albuquerque with his life-partner, Catherine, and their dog, Sophie.

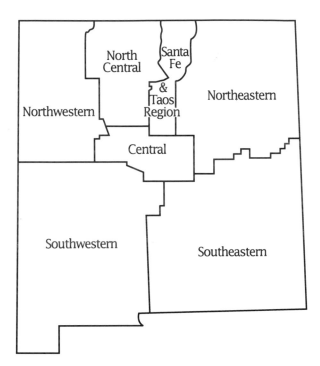

North
Central

Santa
Fe

&
Taos
Region

Northeastern

Northwestern

Central

Southwestern

Southeastern

NEW MEXICO

Contents

Introduction

Renowned New Mexico artist Georgia O'Keeffe once said, "If you ever go to New Mexico, it will itch you for the rest of your life." Millions of folks from all over the world have come to know exactly what she meant. The people, the culture, the landscape, the climate—New Mexico just gets under your skin and takes hold. Whatever form it takes, the New Mexico mystique is a powerful force to reckon with. It may hit you when you're hiking among the ruins of an ancient civilization, strolling along the narrow streets of Santa Fe, or just silently soaking up the smells and sounds of the forest. Frequently visitors become so seduced by The Land of Enchantment that they're compelled to make it their home. When asked why, they can't always explain it. But on a broad scale it has a lot to do with space and freedom and pure light. The ever-present blue skies and spectacular sunsets are also addicting.

Tucked into the southwestern United States, New Mexico itself is essentially off the beaten path. Our state is often confused with Arizona on maps and is even mistaken for the country of Mexico. But most residents cherish this anonymity and obscurity about the place they call home. New Mexico's wide-open spaces, unique history, rich cultural diversity, and endless natural wonders combine to create an ideal atmosphere in which to escape and explore—or even get lost, if that's what you're after.

This is by no means a comprehensive guidebook to New Mexico; there are plenty of good ones around. Rather, it's a selective guide to the state's out-of-the-way treasures—some well known, some not—all of which are unique and offer something special to the adventurous traveler. Geographic diversity and vastness are paramount in New Mexico's 121,330 square miles. The state will delight you with its hidden charms as you explore its ghost towns, quaint bed-and-breakfast inns, quirky cafes, ancient Indian ruins and present-day Indian pueblos, isolated museums, and all the breathtaking scenery you can bear.

While satiating your wanderlust in our expansive state, remember that although New Mexico is the fifth-largest state (after Alaska, Texas, California, and Montana), it ranks thirty-seventh in population—a scant 1.5 million people, of whom approximately a third reside in the Albuquerque metropolitan area. The point: lots of space, few people. Because everything is so spread out, plan some time to get around and always carry a detailed, current map. (Call the New Mexico Department of Economic Development and Tourism, 505–827–0291 or 1–800–545–2040, for a free one.)

As one of the youngest states in the continental United States (it didn't achieve statehood until 1912, though it boasts the oldest capital in the nation, Santa Fe), New Mexico is a land of ancient civilizations. While the Anasazi Indians, ancestors of the state's present-day Pueblo Indians, first occupied parts of New Mexico more than 1,000 years ago, the state is still very much a home to Native Americans. There are nineteen autonomous pueblos (communities on the Indian reservations) inhabited by the different tribes of New Mexico's Pueblo Indians, and part of the Navajo Nation—the largest Indian reservation in the United States—lies in northwestern New Mexico. Native Americans and their rich culture remain a vital part of life in most of our state.

While several pueblos are included as entries in this book, many are not. It's important to realize that the pueblos and reservations do not exist for tourists, though many welcome visitors and even host such events as feast days and ceremonial dances that are open to the public. Keep in mind that the reservations are sovereign nations with their own laws and policies (and languages, though most Native Americans now speak English), so call ahead before you venture out. A list of the Indian tribes of New Mexico is on page 144.

A strong Hispanic heritage also exists in New Mexico. The Spanish first came to New Mexico with Coronado's expedition in 1540, and the first Spanish colony was established near San Juan Pueblo in 1598. Later, additional Spanish settlers came north on El Camino Real ("The Royal Road" connecting Mexico City to Santa Fe). The Spanish influence took hold, and Hispanic traditions and culture are very much inherent in New Mexico. It's this heritage that is also responsible for New Mexico's designation as the oldest wine-growing region in the United States, starting with the missionaries' vineyards in the 1600s. Though a few of the state's many modern wineries are included in this book's narrative, refer to page 147 for a complete list.

New Mexico is also a land of newcomers. Anglo settlers didn't begin arriving until the opening of the Santa Fe Trail in 1821. Later, the railroad connected New Mexico to the population centers of the East. During the early part of this century, Anglo settlers from the East, seeking a remedy for tuberculosis and other ailments, headed to New Mexico's dry climate on their doctors' advice. Many of these latter-day pioneers subsequently made their fortunes here.

New Mexico has also held an allure for artists since the turn of the century. The northern New Mexico community of Taos is a picturesque arts enclave; Santa Fe is firmly established as an art capital of international prominence; and, more recently, Albuquerque too has become known as a major art center. Despite the concentration of galleries in these three cities, small towns throughout the state also offer quality museums and galleries just waiting to be explored.

People often travel the world over without visiting places that have a lasting effect on them, but after your first visit to New Mexico, expect to feel the urge to come back. It was Georgia O'Keeffe's itch, and soon it will be yours as well.

While thorough efforts have been made to verify hours of operation and admission charges and rates, these items often change at the whim of proprietors or as a result of governmental budgets. Therefore, call ahead for current information before traveling.

Off the Beaten Path in Southwestern New Mexico

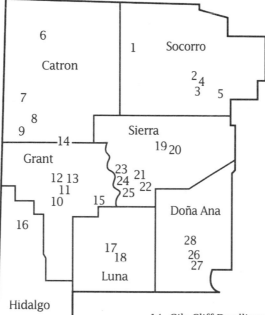

Southwestern New Mexico

This rugged region of the state is often referred to as Old West Country. Its wild-and-woolly past echoes in the remains of ghost towns, museums, and the memories of many old-timers. Mining and ranching have traditionally dominated the landscape and have given residents their fiercely independent nature.

This is also the only region in New Mexico that borders a foreign country—our state's namesake to the south, Mexico. In southwestern New Mexico you'll find the nation's first designated wilderness area, the Gila National Wilderness, as well as our state's largest lake, Elephant Butte. And on a more somber note, this region was the site of the world's first nuclear bomb explosion.

Socorro County

As you approach the **Very Large Array** (VLA, for short) from the east, you'll start to see a pattern of massive white dish-like objects interrupting the grassy plains of the horizon. As you get closer, the picture focuses a bit—"Looks like rows of huge sci-fi ray guns aimed at distant otherworldly enemies," you muse. But at this point, little do you know that the Plains (of San Agustin) are alive with the sounds of outer space.

You can't get more basic or accurate in the naming business than whoever came up with the name of this oft-photographed, high-tech haven: The Very Large Array is a very big deal. Really. The VLA is an astronomical observatory used to study not only our solar system but also distant galaxies at the edge of the universe. Consisting of twenty-seven dish-shaped antennas (each 82 feet in diameter) that are connected to form a single radio telescope, the VLA is the most powerful of its kind in the world. And visiting astronomers from all over the world come here to study the universe.

In the unmanned visitor center a fifteen-minute slide show orients you to the history of the VLA, after which you can check out displays in the museum dedicated to radio astronomy. Next, take the walking-tour trails on the grounds of the

Very Large Array

VLA. One of the first stops is the "Whisper Gallery," where two dishlike structures face each other about 50 feet apart. Have a friend stand at one while you stand at the other. By whispering into a small ball attached to the dish by a string, the two of you can communicate clearly. On a minute and simplified scale, the structure illustrates how the VLA works.

To get to the VLA, drive about 20 miles west of Magdalena via U.S. Highway 60, turn south on Highway 52, and then take a right onto Highway 166 to the visitor center; (505) 772-4255. It's open daily, 8:00 A.M. to sunset, and there's no admission charge.

Clear on the other side of Socorro County, in the small community of San Antonio, you'll find the Owl Bar Cafe & Steak House, commonly known as the **Owl Cafe.** Serving customers since 1945, the Owl Cafe is a watering hole with a reputation—for its green chile cheeseburgers, that is. (Keep in mind that green chile and red chile refer to the peppers that are used extensively in New Mexican cooking. "Chile" with an "e" should never be confused with the bean or meat concoction, "chili.") New Mexicans traveling in these parts make a point to pass through San Antonio around lunchtime just to get their daily chile fix at the cafe.

Choose one of the many booths to get a good view of the old wooden bar that runs the length of the dining area, or, better yet, prop yourself on a bar stool as a vantage point from which to count up all the "wise ones" that constitute the cafe's owl-deco motif. The bar was saved from a fire that destroyed the town's A. H. Hilton Mercantile Store in the early 1940s. It was in Hilton's San Antonio hotel where his son Conrad began as a baggage carrier, only to end up starting one of the world's largest luxury hotel chains years later.

The Owl Cafe is just off I–25 on U.S. Highway 380, about 10 miles south of Socorro; (505) 835–9946. It's open daily except Sunday from 8:00 A.M. to 9:30 P.M. (or 10:00 P.M., if they're busy).

Though you won't find many owls at the **Bosque del Apache** ("Woods of the Apache") **National Wildlife Refuge,** if you time your visit for late fall or winter you're sure to spot lots of migratory birds in this sanctuary along the Rio Grande. Bring plenty of film—and a telephoto lens if you have one—to join the ranks of international photographers who are drawn by the beauty of the *bosque* and its birds.

There's a visitor center that can fill you in on what to expect on the driving or walking tours. The migratory patterns of different bird species are highlighted, and you can put your back against the wall, spread-eagle, in the "How Big Is Your Wingspan?" display to see how you measure up to the feathered ones. Then there's the Birdcall Game, in which you listen to a recorded call and try to match it to a list of birds.

The self-guided, 15-mile Auto Tour Loop takes you through the birds' habitat in the *bosque.* Here's where you get a close view of snow geese, sandhill cranes, peregrine falcons, bald eagles, and the rare whooping cranes, along with 290 other bird species. Don't forget to pack your binoculars—the visitor center doesn't sell or loan them.

Each year during the third weekend in November the refuge hosts the Bosque Fall Festival. It celebrates the wildlife of the Middle Rio Grande Valley and the return of the snow geese and cranes. The festival includes bird-related demonstrations as well as wildlife arts exhibits and area tours.

Bosque del Apache is 8 miles south of Highway 380 (at the Owl Cafe) on Highway 1; (505) 835–1828. There's no admission fee at the visitor center, but there's a $2.00-per-car charge for the auto tour. Visitor center hours are 7:30 A.M.–4:00 P.M. weekdays and 8:00 A.M.–4:30 P.M. weekends. The

Auto Tour Loop opens daily from one hour before sunrise to one hour after sunset.

And if you're a serious birder who just can't get his fill on only a day trip to the *bosque,* book a room at the **Casa Blanca Bed and Breakfast Guesthouse** in San Antonio. Less than 10 miles from Bosque del Apache, the 1880s Victorian country farmhouse is owned by innkeepers John Viebranz and Phoebe Wood. Whether you're into birds or not, a stay at Casa Blanca is a relaxing experience away from the noise of the city.

During the fall and winter, guests enjoy the warmth of wood-burning stoves in both guest rooms and, in warmer times, avail themselves of the rural serenity of Casa Blanca's large veranda surrounding the front of the home. In addition, the bed-and-breakfast has two sitting areas, one with a piano, and one with a large selection of books and board games.

Casa Blanca is a couple of blocks from the Owl Cafe, at 13 Montoya Street in San Antonio; (505) 835–3027. Rates range from $25 to $45.

One of the least accessible and most eerie places in New Mexico is open to the public only twice a year. The **Trinity Site,** ground zero to the world's first nuclear bomb explosion, is located in a remote part of the usually-off-limits White Sands Missile Range deep in southeastern Socorro County. Following more than two years of research and development in Los Alamos (see Los Alamos County entry), the Manhattan Project culminated in the detonation of the bomb at 5:29.45 A.M. on July 16, 1945. The blast was seen across a radius of 160 miles, which included Albuquerque and Santa Fe, and windows were shattered in Silver City, 120 miles from the site.

Most signs of the blast have been removed; even the 1,200-foot-diameter, 8-foot-deep crater resulting from the blast has been filled in. A black lava monument erected in 1965 and a National Historic Landmark plaque dedicated by the National Park Service in 1975 are about all that remain.

The two guided tours are held on the first Saturday in April and October. For information on the Trinity Site tours, call the Alamogordo Chamber of Commerce (1–800–545–4021; in New Mexico, 1–800–826–0294).

Catron County

In the nation's most lightning-struck region sits **Walter de Maria's Lightning Field.** You can't just drop by for the show, though: All visits are overnight affairs and require prior reservations. The Lightning Field is large-scale environmental art created by artist Walter de Maria. The work is composed of four hundred 15- to 20-foot shiny steel poles placed in a grid measuring 1 mile by 3,330 feet. During thunderstorms the poles act as lightning rods, creating a dazzling light show.

The adventure starts in the town of Quemado, where, after meeting with the caretaker early in the afternoon, you're taken for a forty-five-minute ride on dirt roads to a visitor cabin. You, along with any other visitors, are then left until late the next morning. During the day, take the two-hour hike to the field to get a closer look at the rods and wander among them; as long as there's no lightning, you're safe. Otherwise, you can safely view the lightning strikes as long as you stay outside the perimeter of the field.

Because late summer is prime time for thunderstorms, a visit in late July or August gives you the best chance for a spectacular show. The field is also attractive during other times of the year, however, because the shiny rods provide shows of another sort with the help of sunshine or, on a clear night, moonlight.

For more information and to make reservations, call (505) 989-5602. A one-night stay costs $65 per person, which includes meals and transportation to and from Quemado.

As New Mexico's most sparsely populated but geographically largest county, Catron County contains the bulk of the 3-million-acre Gila National Forest. But even though the county seat and largest town, Reserve, has a scant 500 people, you'll find on Reserve's Main Street a mix of old shops, cafes, and bars, as well as **Tularosa Dry Goods,** an Old West mercantile.

Like increasing numbers of easterners, Christie and Ed Cope fell in love with New Mexico during their travels. They thus sold their business in Massachusetts and made the leap out West to open the mercantile. The store, with its rustic wooden doors, walls, and fixtures, is a fun place to browse and pick up a few items you can't find in the big city—or any other place, for that matter.

The store features authentic Old West clothing, not the "country-western" attire worn by the singing set of Nashville. We're talking late 1800s duds worn by the pioneering men and women of New Mexico, Colorado, Wyoming, and Montana—the real West. Beaver felt hats made by local hatter Butch Dorer share space with blue jeans patterned after Levi Strauss's 1890 designs. Chaps, suspenders, leather goods, blue-speck enamelware, cooking irons, and handwoven saddle blankets are just some of the merchandise on display.

The store is near the junction of Highway 12 and U.S. Highway 180 on Main Street; (505) 533–6830. It's open Tuesday through Saturday, 10:00 a.m.–5:00 P.M.

The picturesque ghost town of **Mogollon** is set in a narrow valley flanked by canyon walls along Silver Creek. For about sixty years after its great gold strike of 1878, Mogollon earned a reputation for lawlessness as the Mogollon Mountains continued to give up millions of dollars worth of gold, silver, and copper. Perhaps because of its inaccessibility, neither territorial troops nor the Apache warriors Victorio and Geronimo could tame this onetime headquarters of Butch Cassidy and his crew.

Today Mogollon is only semighostly: A handful of residents live here, and the old buildings are only slightly marred by the presence of facades built for the 1973 western *My Name Is Nobody,* starring Henry Fonda. Mogollon is, however, still one of New Mexico's most well-preserved ghost towns. During the summer, a couple of residents open shops for the trickle of visitors who venture into these parts.

Mogollon is located about 9 miles east of U.S. Highway 180 (about 37 miles south of Reserve) on Highway 159—a very narrow, rough, cliff-hugging road with many hairpin turns. (It is paved, though.)

About 3½ miles farther south on U.S. Highway 180 you'll come across the tiny village of Glenwood. It's here where you can explore one of the truly awesome sites in New Mexico: the **Mogollon Catwalk.** Plan this outing in late fall or early winter, during the week if possible, to avoid seeing another soul. You can't find a better site for a picnic.

Set in the beautiful Whitewater Canyon just outside Glenwood, the Catwalk trailhead is covered with stately old sycamores and cottonwoods. The perfectly clear Whitewater Creek rushes alongside the trail, completing the pristine setting. The canyon was a favorite hideout for Apaches and desperados, including Butch Cassidy, in the 1880s.

The initial rocky trail soon turns into the Catwalk, a narrow metal walkway (with a sturdy rail) that hugs the sheer-rock wall of the gorge as it winds along the creek up the canyon for about 1 mile past the gorge. Though the gorge is 100 feet deep (and the canyon walls rise 1,400 feet), the Catwalk stays about 20 feet above the river. The point is that a walk on the Catwalk is exciting and visually stimulating, but it's not scary. The Catwalk is well maintained for safety.

The Catwalk got its start as the result of pipelines that were laid through the canyon in 1893 to provide water for a mill that serviced nearby gold and silver claims. Because the lines needed continual maintenance, the workers who had to walk along the suspended pipes referred to them as the catwalk. Today you can even see parts of the old pipelines.

The Mogollon Catwalk is located about 5 miles from U.S. Highway 180 in Glenwood (40 miles south of Reserve), at the end of Highway 174 (well marked with signs). There are no set hours, admission charges, or phones.

The best place to stay in Catron County is Los Olmos Guest Ranch in Glenwood, a bargain when you consider that the $65–$80 rate for a couple includes both breakfast and dinner. Besides the cabins, available are a pool, a saloon, and fishing. A fish hatchery, practically next door, is also an interesting diversion. Los Olmos is located near the intersection of U.S. Highway 180 and Highway 174; (505) 539–2311. It closes for the winter.

Grant County

Silver City is the largest city in Grant County and home of Western New Mexico University. As its name implies, mining played a key role in the town's history. Billy the Kid also figures into Silver City's past—he spent part of his childhood here before moving on to establish his notoriously lawless life.

Unlike most of New Mexico's old mining towns, Silver City survived the boom-bust pattern of the industry to become Grant County's trade center and county seat. At the turn of the century, the town capitalized on its dry climate to become a haven for people with tuberculosis. This delightful climate, with its four distinct seasons, continues to attract new residents, particularly retirees.

Take a stroll down Bullard Street (around Broadway Street) near the city's center to check out its historic downtown district. You'll find an eclectic mix of shops and cafes housed in architecturally significant, late 1800s buildings. Like Las Vegas, New Mexico, up north (see San Miguel County entry), Silver City's inner core is enhanced by a choice selection of Victorian homes.

One of the city's finest examples of Victorian architecture is now the home of the **Silver City Museum.** But this unusual brick structure was originally the home of mining magnate Harry Ailman, who had it built in 1881. Later it served as the city hall and as a fire station before becoming a museum in 1967. This is the place to start investigating Silver City's rich history, from the prehistoric Mogollon Indians who inhabited the area, through the mining days, to the present. The museum sponsors special, long-running exhibits, such as "More Than Civilizers: Women of Silver City, 1870–1910." Visitors can even climb to the top in the museum's cupola, built for ventilation, and get a 360-degree view of the town.

The Silver City Museum is located at 312 West Broadway; (505) 538–5921. It's open Tuesday through Friday from 9:00 A.M. to 4:30 P.M. and weekends from 10:00 A.M. to 4:00 P.M. There's no admission charge.

Just north of Silver City, on the edge of the Gila National Forest, the village of **Pinos Altos** ("Tall Pines") is a prime spot for any off-the-beaten-pather. Though Pinos Altos's mining history dates from 1803, it was a later gold discovery by three Forty-Niners from California in 1860 that led to the establishment of Pinos Altos as a mining camp. Roy Bean operated a general store here with his brother before moving to Texas to become "the law west of the Pecos." During the past few years, several of the town's old stores have been replaced by modern shops.

Pinos Altos's points of interest include the **Hearst Church,** the Buckhorn Saloon, and the Pinos Altos Museum. The near-century-old Hearst Church was built with money donated by Phoebe Hearst, whose late husband, George (father of William Randolph Hearst), had left her mining interests in Pinos Altos. The small adobe church, originally called the Gold Avenue Methodist Episcopal Church, now houses the Grant County Art Guild. It also contains the hearse that carried the body of Pat Garrett (killer of Billy the Kid), along with other horse-drawn vehicles. Unfortunately, the church is not kept open regular hours.

With its faded whitewashed facade, the **Buckhorn Saloon** is one of the West's finest old bars, distinguished by 18-inch-thick adobe walls and rustic timbers. Stepping through the old watering hole's doors at dusk is like stepping back a hundred years. The saloon glows with soft lighting and smiling people clustered around the bar and small tables. The Buckhorn now also has a fine restaurant.

On closer inspection, two perennial bar patrons aren't even real—they're realistic-looking mannequins. Indian Joe keeps his seat at one end of the bar; though occasionally a newcomer offers to buy him a drink, he's yet to acknowledge the offer. Debbie DeCamp, the other mannequin, keeps an eye on the saloon entrance from a balcony; she's based on a young woman who lived in Pinos Altos at the turn of the century and met an untimely death during a brawl. A friend, the story goes, wrote the following "memorial" over the door to Debbie's room:

> Shed a tear for Debbie DeCamp,
> Born a virgin and died a tramp.
> For 17 years she retained her virginity.
> (A real good record for this vicinity.)

The Pinos Altos Museum, just across the road from the Buckhorn, details the village's history. The tin-roofed log cabin was the county's first private schoolhouse, built around 1866.

Pinos Altos is located about 6 miles north of Silver City, just off Highway 15. Be aware that once you're in Pinos Altos, most of the roads are dirt but are in good condition unless there's been a lot of rain.

Deep within the Gila National Forest but less than 40 miles farther on Highway 15, you'll find the rather hidden **Gila Cliff Dwellings National Monument** (505–536–9344). It's dedicated to preserving and celebrating the ancient Pueblo Indians of the Mogollon culture who inhabited the area for about a hundred years starting around 1280. These cliff dwellers were approximate contemporaries of the Anasazi Indians who lived in New Mexico's northwestern region. Similar to the Anasazi, the Mogollon Indians mysteriously disappeared, and archaeologists have been puzzled ever since the dwellings were discovered. Drought, disease, or tribal wars top the list of theories.

A visit to the park involves a healthy mile's hike along a trail that ascends some 200 feet up the canyon walls to the cliff dwellings. The dwellings themselves are tucked into caves in the cliff and are made of adobe and timber. Most visitors are extremely quiet when walking among the rooms of the dwellings, partly because the caves' acoustics amplify voices but also because they're showing respect for the people who lived here so long ago. On the edge of the Gila National Wilderness, the monument is a peaceful and beautiful place for the hike.

The Gila Cliff Dwellings are open daily 8:00 A.M.– 6:00 P.M. (visitor center, 8:00 A.M.–5:00 P.M.) Memorial Day through Labor Day and 9:00 A.M.–4:00 P.M. (visitor center, 8:00 A.M.– 4:30 P.M.) the rest of the year. There's no admission charge. (*Note:* The park itself is actually in Catron County but is accessible only through Grant County.)

Heading southeast of Silver City toward Deming you'll find **City of Rocks State Park.** This relatively flat park is filled with vertical rock formations, some as high as 50 feet, resembling the monoliths at Stonehenge. The rocks are the result of erosion on the remains of volcanic eruptions occurring millions of years ago. Because you can climb on the rocks, as well as hide behind them, this park is a natural playground for kids of all ages. Picnic and camping facilities are available. The park is located 31 miles southeast of Silver City via U.S. Highway 180 and Highway 61; (505) 536–2800. It's open daily, from 7:00 A.M. to sunset. Admission is $3.00 per vehicle.

Hidalgo County

Texas and Oklahoma may have their panhandles, but New Mexico's got its bootheel and Hidalgo County is it. Closer to Tucson, Arizona, than to Albuquerque, most of this area is desolate, although cattle ranching and, more recently, vineyards have made their imprint on the land. The largest town is Lordsburg, but perhaps the most unique place is **Shakespeare,** a ghost town 2½ miles southwest of Lordsburg.

Originally settled in the 1850s as Mexican Springs, a stage stop on the Butterfield Overland Trail, the name Shakespeare was selected in 1879 by mine promoters to honor the bard and perhaps to improve the town's fortunes. The town was the site of a couple of mining hoaxes including the Diamond Swindle of 1870—in which the area was seeded with diamonds to attract investors—before a real silver boom hit in 1879, only to fizzle some fifteen years later. Shakespeare's last hurrah came with a second silver strike in 1907. The silver played out in the 1930s.

Because the town has been privately owned since 1935, it's been protected from weekend ghost-town looters, and the admission charge goes toward further preservation and restoration. It's accessible to the public only through guided tours that include the interiors of several buildings. One of these structures, the Stratford Hotel, is said to have briefly employed Billy the Kid as a dishwasher.

To get to Shakespeare, take the Main Street exit off I-10 in Lordsburg, turn south, and follow the signs. Tours are held at 10:00 A.M. and 2:00 P.M. on the second and fourth Saturday and Sunday of the month, January through October; call (505) 542–9034 to verify the current year's dates. The admission charge is $2.00.

Luna County

Luna County's primary community is Deming, known for its pure air and fast ducks. Yes, ducks. Deming is home of the world-famous Great American Duck Race, held annually the fourth weekend in August. Thought up more than ten years ago in a bar as a way to create more interest in the area, the duck races have captured international media coverage for Deming. More than just a duck race, the grand event includes a parade, a golf tournament, a chile cookoff, a hot-air-balloon rally, several sporting tournaments, and even a "Duck Queen" contest. It's also become one of New Mexico's most well-attended events.

Deming's more than ducks, though. The city's also home to the impressive **Deming Luna Mimbres Museum.** Located in the 3-story, 1916 red-brick National Guard Armory building, the museum has about 25,000 square feet of exhibition space. There's a bit of everything here, as evidenced by the many "theme rooms," including the Military Room, the Quilt Room, the Doll Room, and the Tack Room. The museum also depicts life in the Southwest, focusing on ranching, railroading, and mining. The Mimbres Room showcases examples of centuries-old Mimbres Indian pottery. The pottery's distinctive, black-on-white geometric designs are known for the way they mismatch animal body parts.

The museum is at 301 South Silver in Deming; (505) 546-2382. It's open Monday through Saturday from 9:00 A.M.–4:00 P.M., and Sunday from 1:30–4:00 P.M. There's no set admission charge, but nominal contributions are expected.

Most parks make a big deal about leaving everything as you found it and strictly forbid visitors to take anything with them when they leave. But at **Rockhound State Park,** located on the west side of the Little Florida Mountains, "taking a little of the park" is encouraged. That's right—visitors may each take up to fifteen pounds of rocks with them per visit. You'll find all kinds and colors here, including varieties of quartz crystals, agates, and opals. Even after years of rock hounds carrying away mementos of their visit, old-timers say it's hard to tell that the place is any different from how it was years ago. Plan to spend a lot of time staring at the ground here, and while you're on the lookout for your personal gems watch out as well for loose rock and inconspicuous drop-offs.

Rockhound State Park is off Palomas Road via Highway 11, southeast of Deming; (505) 546-6182. It's open daily, from 7:30 A.M. to sunset. There's a $3.00-per-vehicle admission charge.

Sierra County

Sierra County is home to New Mexico's largest body of water, Elephant Butte Lake. It's named for a huge gray rock formation, or butte, which rises from the water and resembles an elephant. Near the lake you'll come across the city of **Truth or Consequences.** The city changed its name from Hot Springs to Truth or Consequences in 1951, following an open challenge over the airwaves from the popular radio show of the same name to honor its tenth anniversary. As a reward for the name change, the show pledged the city an annual festival during which the show would be broadcast. The show, along with its later television incarnation, has long since ended, but the annual Truth or Consequences Fiesta is still going strong. And Ralph Edwards, former host of the show, hasn't missed one yet.

Truth or Consequences (often "T or C," for short—an abbreviation locals don't particularly care for) is popular for its many therapeutic hot springs (from which the community got its first name). The town's even got a trade association for those businesses that still cater to people who appreciate a good soak.

Near the town's center, you'll find **Geronimo Springs Museum,** named after a spring frequented by Geronimo, the famous Apache war chief. The spring has been "modernized" with the addition of a circular enclosure and a roof, but you can still see and hear it bubbling around the rocks.

The museum is one of those community types for which residents have donated a broad assortment of artifacts from the area's past. The museum is laid out according to four categories: the Historical Past, Natural Resources, Ralph Edwards and the Fiesta, and the Cultural Heritage Room. This last space really takes visitors by surprise, with its floor-to-ceiling murals of famous locals painted by noted muralist Delmas Howe, who was born in Truth or Consequences. The room also contains four bronze statues of other famous New Mexicans, each sculpted by Hivana Leyendecker, an accomplished native New Mexican artist.

The museum is located on Main Street across from the post office; (505) 894–6600. It's open Monday through Saturday, 9:00 A.M.–5:00 P.M. Admission charges are $1.50 for adults and 75 cents for children over five.

Southwest of Truth or Consequences, the village of Hillsboro is the quintessential one-horse town. Established in 1877 as the result of a gold discovery in the hills surrounding Percha Creek, Hillsboro is perfect for just pulling off the main street and strolling around town. You'll find several antiques shops, a couple of galleries, a general store, an old saloon, and the Black Range Museum. Hillsboro is the kind of place where all the townspeople and merchants know one another and where a few well-cared-for "community" dogs take naps in the middle of Main Street. Steeped in mining history, the town is an enchanting, slow-paced marvel that has lured more than its share of artists and writers to become residents.

Speaking of enchanting, the **Enchanted Villa Bed & Breakfast** (505–895–5686) has a home along Hillsboro's main street. Run by innkeeper Maree Westland, this large, bright, white-washed home was designed by Maree's aunt in 1941 as a romantic retreat for English nobleman Sir Victor Sassoon. The 2-story inn's five large guest rooms all have lots of well-positioned windows for maximum light, and there are antiques and oak floors throughout. Rates range from $45 to $90.

The **Hillsboro General Store** deserves more than a casual mention. This is the real thing. Continuously open since 1879, the store has survived boom and bust while serving as a post office, stage stop, telegraph office, soda fountain, and phone company. Though it still stocks most things the rural household needs at a moment's notice, these days most folks visit the store when they're hungry. A large part of the store is now the Country Cafe and serves up hearty breakfasts and lunches featuring soups, sandwiches, burgers, and a few New Mexican selections.

Hillsboro is 30 miles from Truth or Consequences: 12 miles south on I–25 and then 18 miles west on Highway 152.

Nine miles farther west on Highway 152, you'll enter the Black Range of the Mimbres Mountains in **Kingston,** a blink-and-you'll-miss-it community—so check your odometer and don't blink. Kingston, population 30, is pretty much deserted now, though a tiny museum is housed in the old Percha Valley Bank building and the original schoolhouse is used as the meeting place for the Spit and Whittle Club. Kingston's history mirrors Hillsboro's, and it certainly saw more prosperous days during the silver boom of the 1880s, when the population soared to 7,000.

Hillsboro General Store

The 3-story, ivy-covered **Black Range Lodge** stands as testimony to those earlier days. Run by Hollywood escapees and filmmakers/innkeepers Catherine Wanek and Mike Sherlock, the lodge is now a bed-and-breakfast with the feel of an Old West boardinghouse. It's one of the few bed-and-breakfasts that welcome pets—a great relief when the kennel fills up at the last minute and Rover needs a weekend getaway just as much as you do.

The innkeepers' background in the entertainment business is evident in the large common area of the lodge's second floor. Those who need more stimulation will find a pool table, a cassette deck, a satellite-television-and-VCR-system complete with videotape library, and video games. For those who do, however, appreciate the tranquillity of the lodge's natural setting, hunting for crystals along the rocky trails near the inn is a relaxing pastime—sort of like hunting for seashells on the beach.

If you find Kingston, you'll find the Black Range Lodge—trust me; (505) 895–5652. Rates range from $30 to $50.

While staying at the lodge, take a break from your hiking adventures by visiting **Sarah's Closet Coffee House and Gift Shop,** located just up the street from the lodge. It's the only place to get something to eat in Kingston, and Sarah makes great sandwiches and made-from-scratch pies. Because this is by no means a high-traffic town, Sarah's is open only on weekends and on request for guests of the Black Range Lodge.

Doña Ana County

Doña Ana County is home to New Mexico's second-largest city, Las Cruces ("The Crosses"), which in turn is home to New Mexico's second-largest college, New Mexico State University. Located in the fertile Mesilla Valley between the Organ Mountains and the Rio Grande, Las Cruces hosts the Whole Enchilada Festival each October, culminating in the cooking of the world's largest enchilada.

Fine art and hospitality meet at **Lundeen Inn of the Arts,** the most distinctive place to stay in the Las Cruces area. Run by Linda and Jerry Lundeen, this bed-and-breakfast adjoins Linda's gallery and Jerry's architectural office, but it's hard to tell where one begins and the other ends. Works by southwestern artists are everywhere, including the guest rooms. And since most of it's for sale, if you have fond memories of your stay in a particular room you can arrange to take a piece of it home. Then again, if you've always wondered what's entailed in making adobe bricks, Jerry might just give you a lesson, time permitting. Once you find out the process, you'll understand why real adobe homes are so expensive, in comparison with stucco-covered-concrete homes passed off as adobe.

The inn was formed by joining two historic adobe homes by a great room that has a soaring ceiling. In addition to being the place where breakfast is served, this naturally lighted common area is the focal point for much of the inn's art. Each of the fifteen oversize guest rooms is unique in both configuration and decor and is named after an American artist, such as Georgia O'Keeffe and R. C. Gorman. All

17

rooms have queen-size beds and private baths, while some even have fireplaces and limited kitchen facilities, convenient for long-term guests.

The inn is located at 618 South Alameda; (505) 526–3327. Rates range from $50 to $75.

Although a separate community, **Mesilla** (alternately La Mesilla or Old Mesilla) connects to the southwest side of Las Cruces. This rural "part" of Las Cruces played an important role in the history of New Mexico. The Gadsden Purchase— which annexed Mesilla to the United States from Mexico and established the current international borders of New Mexico and Arizona—was signed here in 1854. Mesilla is also the place where Billy the Kid was convicted of murder, sentenced to hang, and jailed for a short time in 1881. The village was even briefly declared the Confederate capital of a territory extending all the way to California. The tree-lined Old Mesilla Plaza is anchored by the San Albino Church and is surrounded by uncluttered shops and restaurants; it's a great place to visit on an autumn Saturday afternoon. Just across Highway 28 from Old Mesilla Plaza on Calle del Parian, you'll find the Gadsden Museum, which displays Indian, Civil War, and Old West artifacts.

Heading north on I–25 out of Las Cruces, you'll come across **Fort Selden State Monument.** The now-abandoned adobe military fort that contributed to the growth of Las Cruces was one of many forts built in the mid-1800s to protect settlers and travelers from Apache Indian attacks. It was the boyhood home of General Douglas MacArthur from 1884 to 1886, when his father was the post commander; moreover, the acclaimed Buffalo Soldiers, a regiment of black soldiers honored for their success in subduing the Plains Indians, were also stationed here.

A visitor center explains the history of the fort and displays articles of interest found here. Outside, you can walk along the trails that wind about the adobe ruins. Interspersed along the trail are interpretive signs whose replicas of old photos show the fort as it was in the 1800s.

The monument is located 15 miles north of Las Cruces off I–25. Take the Radium Springs exit and head west a couple of miles; (505) 526–8911. It's open May through September 15 from 9:30 A.M. to 5:30 P.M. and September 16 through April 30 from 8:30 A.M. to 4:30 P.M. The admission charge is $2.00, while children under sixteen are admitted free.

Though the place is beyond the scope of this book, off-the-beaten-pathers should keep in mind that the Mexican city of Juárez is only 44 miles from Las Cruces, just across the border from El Paso, Texas. And you don't even need a passport to cross. You'll find great native food, potent margaritas, and bargain shopping galore.

Off the Beaten Path in Northwestern New Mexico

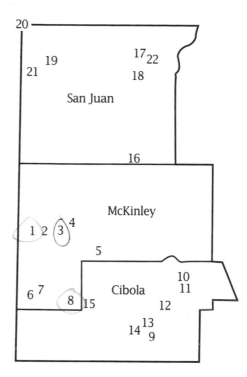

1. Gallup
2. Richardson's Trading Post
3. El Rancho Hotel
4. Red Rock State Park
5. Carol Sayre Gallery
6. Zuni Pueblo
7. Mission Church of Nuestra Señora de Guadalupe
8. Vogt Ranch Bed and Breakfast
9. Acoma Pueblo
10. Shrine of Los Portales
11. Don José's Cocina
12. New Mexico Museum of Mining
13. El Malpais National Monument and Conservation Area
14. Candelaria Ice Cave and Bandera Crater
15. El Morro National Monument
16. Chaco Culture National Historical Park
17. Aztec Ruins National Monument
18. Salmon Ruin
19. Hogback Trading Post
20. Four Corners Monument
21. Shiprock
22. Aztec Historic District

Northwestern New Mexico

Because of its large population of Native Americans, north-western New Mexico proudly bears the name Indian Country. Part of the Navajo Nation—the largest Indian reservation in the United States—is located in this region, as are the Zuni, Acoma, Ramah Navajo, and Laguna reservations. The vast juniper-dotted mesas and multihued rock formations will leave you in awe, especially if you're an urban dweller. It's a great place to just wander for a few hours or even a few days.

The three counties composing this region are huge, so notable attractions are often widely scattered in this sparsely populated region. Look closely at the mileage scale on your trusty map and come along to discover some of the special spots in northwestern New Mexico.

McKinley County

Named after David L. Gallup, a paymaster for the Atlantic and Pacific Railroad, the city of **Gallup** was founded in 1881. Situated near the Arizona border along old Route 66, Gallup thrives in the heart of Indian Country. The Navajo and Zuni Indians swell this small town's population to more than 100,000 on weekends, when they come to town to trade.

Most everything in Gallup is located along its main street (alternately Highway 118 and East or West 66 Avenue), a healthy stretch of old Route 66, "America's Mother Road," which was stripped of its legendary identity when I–40 homogenized its path in the 1960s. Gallup's downtown main strip is lined with its own brand of distinctive pawnshops. Whereas in most cities pawnshops are seen as seedy places of last resort for desperate borrowers, in Gallup this image couldn't be further from reality. In addition to providing ready markets for Indian wares, Gallup's pawnshops act as financial institutions for many Native Americans. An advanced system of barter and credit has evolved over the years.

The pawnshops are veritable museums of Indian jewelry and other artifacts. Display cases and vaults gleam with turquoise and silver. If you want a good deal on authentic Indian arts and crafts, including jewelry, here's the place to buy. Retailers come from all over to Gallup to buy Indian wares, which they then sell elsewhere—at a sizable markup. A favorite of Native Americans and others since 1918, **Richardson's Trading Post** is perhaps the best place to view the trade, as well as to get a great price from a reputable dealer with a wide selection. Located at 222 West 66 Avenue (505–722–4762), Richardson's is open Monday through Saturday, 9:00 A.M.–6:00 P.M.

East of downtown, the notable **El Rancho Hotel** commands attention from passing motorists. In 1987 the well-known Indian trader Armand Ortega bought the historic property, as it was threatened with demolition. After extensive renovations, the hotel reopened in May 1988.

Originally built in 1937 by the brother of movie mogul D. W. Griffith, the El Rancho became known as a Hollywood hideaway in the 1940s and 1950s. Scores of actors were drawn to Gallup by the many films (mostly Westerns) made in the area. Spencer Tracy, Katharine Hepburn, Humphrey Bogart, Rita Hayworth, and Ronald Reagan all stayed at the hotel. Restored to its former rustic glamour, the hotel's 2-story lobby is lined with autographed photos of Hollywood's brightest stars of the era who stayed at the El Rancho.

The El Rancho is located at 1000 East 66 Avenue; (505) 863–9311. Room rates range from $32 for a single in the motel section to $65 for a two-bedroom suite in the original hotel.

Red Rock State Park, minutes from the center of town, is a wonderful place to explore. Red Rock Museum, located in the park, showcases area artifacts from the Ice Age to the present, and rare Indian arts and crafts are also on display. The museum's garden areas identify the plants native to the high mesa region. The park itself, with its exquisite crimson cliffs, is one of New Mexico's top nonforest spots for camping. If you want solitude, however, visit during the week. For good weather without the crowds, plan your stay during early spring and late fall.

Red Rock State Park is off Highway 566 via Highway 118 or I–40, about 10 miles east of Gallup; (505) 722-6196. The museum is open daily from 8:00 A.M. to 9:00 P.M. Memorial Day through Labor Day and Monday through Friday from

8:00 A.M. to 4:30 P.M. the remainder of the year. Admission charges are $1.00 for adults and 50 cents for children.

The park hosts the annual Inter-Tribal Ceremonial (ITC). Held each year since 1922, the ITC includes an all-Indian rodeo, an arts and crafts show, and the ceremonial dances of many tribes throughout the West, from Canada to Mexico. The four-day ITC begins the second Thursday in August and is known as the largest Indian gathering of its kind in the world. The ITC Association can be reached at (505) 863-3896.

Halfway between Gallup and the city of Grants (see Cibola County entry), you'll find the tiny community of Thoreau located near the Continental Divide, the demarcation separating streams that flow to opposite sides of North America. (Though probably named after writer Henry David Thoreau, the name of the town is pronounced "through.") Thoreau sits at the juncture of I-40 and Highway 371 and is home to the highly respected **Carol Sayre Gallery.** Though a little rougher around the edges than the big-city art galleries in Albuquerque, Santa Fe, and Taos, Carol Sayre Gallery exhibits the works of some of the Southwest's best-known artists. Carol and her husband, Jim, a retired rodeo bull rider and sculptor, run the gallery and sculpture garden.

Carol Sayre Gallery is located on Red Hills Road in Thoreau (unfortunately, there's no road sign, but if you take the Thoreau exit off I-40, signs will direct you to the gallery); (505) 862-7550. Someone's almost always there during the daylight hours, but it's best to call ahead to make sure.

About 38 miles south of Gallup you'll come across **Zuni Pueblo,** New Mexico's largest Indian pueblo, with a population of about 9,000. Zuni's isolation from New Mexico's Rio Grande–situated pueblos makes its history, culture, and language unique.

The Zuni people have occupied the area of the reservation for more than 1,700 years. Their ancestors played an important role in the early recorded history of the Southwest. In search of the Seven Cities of Cibola—the fabled cities of gold—Spanish explorers first discovered Zuni in 1539. Encouraged by persistent rumors (as well as Indian fabrications to persuade the Spaniards to go elsewhere in search of the gold), more explorers, including Coronado, followed but failed to find riches.

In 1629 the Spanish established **Mission Church of Nues-tra Señora de Guadalupe** (also known as the Old Mission) at Zuni. The church was restored in 1970, and internationally known Zuni artist and muralist Alex Seowtewa began painting his colorful murals on the interior of the church walls. Seowtewa's work has drawn some famous admirers to Zuni, among them Jackie Onassis and Mother Teresa. Seowtewa continues work on the murals with the assistance of his son Kenneth and a grant from the National Endowment for the Arts. Call the tribal offices at (505) 782–4481 for updated viewing hours at the Old Mission.

The pueblo has several shops where you may purchase Zuni-made arts including stone- and shell-carved fetishes (birds and other animals used since prehistoric times for luck in hunting and fertility in crops) and the turquoise petit point and needle point jewelry for which the pueblo is famous. Zuni is located on Highway 53, via Highway 602, about 38 miles south of Gallup.

The **Vogt Ranch Bed and Breakfast** is probably the most secluded inn in New Mexico and is one of the nicest for its authentic period furnishings and privacy. That the innkeeper doesn't live in the bed-and-breakfast is a nice treat for those of us who like an attentive but distant host.

Although the inn has been open to the public for only a few years, innkeeper Anita Davis carries on the Vogt family tradition of frontier living. Her grandfather, Evon Zartman Vogt, left his studies at the University of Chicago in 1906 to move West for health reasons and later married and brought back a wife, Shirley, to the ranch. He established the Vogt Sheep Company and was in the ranching business for twenty-one years, later serving as superintendent of nearby El Morro National Monument (see Cibola County entry).

In 1915, Vogt built his family's home (now the inn) out of rocks from nearby Indian ruins—something that would make present-day anthropologists cringe. Over the years the Vogt family hosted many visitors, including artists, writers, anthropologists, and archaeologists.

Anita has kept the Vogt home just the way her grandmother left it upon her death in 1986. The place is complete with a piano brought from Chicago in 1915, old Navajo rugs (some of which had been used as horse blankets!), a bear pelt on the wall, and artifacts from Grandfather Vogt's sheepherding days. The two guest rooms have private baths and phones, but there's not a television in sight; instead, visitors have use of an extensive collection of books, many signed by their authors.

Though a stay at Vogt Ranch includes a full breakfast (often with blue-corn pancakes and muffins), finding other meals may be more of a challenge. Other than the Stagecoach Inn cafe, about 1 mile west in the community of Ramah, restaurants are distant—Gallup, 40 miles; Grants, 54 miles; and Zuni Pueblo, 21 miles. It might be a good idea to bring a wine-and-cheese assortment of picnic food just in case you want to stay in.

The Vogt Ranch is located 21 miles east of Zuni Pueblo on Highway 53 (10 miles west of El Morro National Monument if you're coming from Grants); (505) 783–4362. Rates range from $42 to $55. The inn is closed January through March.

Cibola County

Acoma Pueblo, or "Sky City," as it's sometimes called, is the oldest continuously inhabited community in the United States: Archaeologists have traced the pueblo's occupation to 1150. But it wasn't until 1540 that the Spanish explorer Coronado became the first non-Indian to enter Acoma, and outsiders have been fascinated with Sky City ever since.

The pueblo, located on a 367-foot mesa on the Acoma Indian Reservation outside Grants, operates a visitor center that includes a museum and gift shops at the base of the mesa. Guided tours of Acoma—the only way outsiders can view the pueblo—are offered hourly from the visitor center every day, with the exception of three private ceremonial periods. Small buses provide transportation to the top of the mesa, and from there an Acoma guide will point out the various elements of the pueblo while filling you in on Acoma's long and colorful history. The mesa-top pueblo provides stunning views of the surrounding area, including the spectacular 400-foot-tall Enchanted Mesa, said to be the home of the ancestral Acomas.

The singularly most impressive structure in the pueblo is

Enchanted Mesa

Mission San Esteban Del Rey, a church completed in 1640 after eleven years of intense labor by Acoma residents. The massive roof beams were carried from the forests of Mount Taylor, 40 miles away—without ever touching the logs to the ground, according to Acoma legend. The church, whose adobe walls are 7 to 9 feet thick, has no windows, because it was used as a fortress.

Even though the pueblo has no electricity or running water, about twelve families live here; most Acoma Pueblo Indians, however, live in communities nearby. Some of the pueblo residents sell their world-famous, intricately designed pottery during tours, and often you can purchase bread baked in the beehive-shaped *hornos,* or adobe ovens, that dot the pueblo. The tour guide will also point out and explain the use of kivas, or sacred ceremonial chambers; note, though, that entrance to kivas is strictly prohibited for visitors.

To get to the visitor center from Grants, head east on I–40, take exit 96, and follow the signs to the visitor center; (505) 252-1139. From Albuquerque, head west on I–40 (about 55 miles), take exit 108, and do the same. Tours are held as follows: fall and winter, 8:00 A.M.–4:00 P.M.; spring, 8:00 A.M.–6:00 P.M.; and summer, 8:00 A.M.–7:00 P.M. Each year tours cease July 10–13, Easter weekend, and either the first or second weekend in October (it varies). Tour admission is $5.00 for adults, $4.00 for senior citizens, and $3.00 for children. Camera and sketching fees apply, and there are photographic restrictions. There's no admission fee for the visitor center and museum, however.

The **Shrine of Los Portales** lies in a hidden grotto near the old Spanish land-grant village of Syboyeta (sometimes spelled Cebolleta on maps), north of Laguna Pueblo and east of the city of Grants. A statue of St. Bernadette of Lourdes is the focal point of the beautiful, mysterious shrine.

Brought from Spain, the original statue for the shrine, *Our Lady of Sorrows,* is now protected in the mission church of the same name in Syboyeta. The legend goes that during one of the last Navajo raids in the 1800s, the women and children took refuge in the natural fortress while the men were away. The women vowed that if their husbands and sons returned safely, the women would build a shrine to the Virgin Mary at which to hold an annual mass.

The shallow cave or overhang of the rounded cliff that forms the large semicircular enclave is perfect for meditation or prayer, as evidenced by the many melted candles that can be seen at the shrine. Weatherworn wooden pews face the shrine at an angle. Spring water, considered holy, seeps from the cliff and collects in several small pools. Because of the abundance of moisture, this protected area is unusually green and forms a small oasis that contrasts with the barren land of the surrounding region.

Syboyeta is on Highway 279, off Highway 124, which connects to I–40 near Laguna Pueblo. To get to the shrine proceed on the main road to Our Lady of Sorrows church at the center of town. Continue winding around the church as the paved road turns to dirt. After $\frac{1}{10}$ mile, turn left and continue for 1 mile until you see a very large tree with exposed roots around its base; the approximately 100-yard trail to the shrine begins here. (*Note:* If there's been a lot of rain, do not attempt this trek unless you have a four-wheel-drive vehicle.)

After a visit to Syboyeta, stop at **Don José's Cocina** in

Ladders at Acoma Pueblo

neighboring Bibo. Pauline Michael opened the restaurant at her family's old homestead in 1978 and serves up fantastic, made-from-scratch New Mexican food at bargain prices. Blue-corn tamales, enchiladas, and *carne adovada* (baked pork that's been marinated in red chile) are some of the favorites. The most expensive combination dinner on the menu is $5.25. Don José's is on Highway 279 in Bibo (you passed right in front of the restaurant on your way to Syboyeta—look for the large Schlitz beer sign on the attached bar); (505) 552–6726. It's open Monday through Friday, 11:00 A.M.–8:00 P.M.

Heading west on I–40 you'll soon be in Grants, the largest town and county seat of Cibola County. Grants's past as a classic Route 66 town is preserved with 1950s-era motels, shops, and cafes along the main strip, now called Santa Fe Avenue. Just off Santa Fe Avenue you'll find the **New Mexico**

Museum of Mining at 100 Iron Street (505–287–4802)—though it was uranium, not iron, that put Grants on the map. The first floor of the museum traces the history of uranium mining in the area from 1950, the year Paddy Martinez, an Indian laborer and occasional prospector, discovered a mother lode of the dusty yellow rock.

The best part of the museum is the underground portion called Section 26, an eerily accurate reproduction of a working uranium mine. You start by taking an elevator down the mine "shaft." Although you don't travel very far, it feels as though you're hundreds of feet below the earth's surface. The tour utilizes hand-held listening devices that explain the exhibits at scheduled stops. Adding to the realism are artifacts from working mines that fill the space—right down to the tool company "girlie calendar" in the miners' lunchroom.

The New Mexico Museum of Mining is open Monday through Friday, 10:00 A.M.–12:00 noon and 1:00–4:00 P.M.; Saturday, 10:00 A.M–4:00 P.M.; and Sunday, 1:00–4:00 P.M. Admission is $2.00.

Highway 53, which connects Grants with Zuni Pueblo (see McKinley County entry), is the most scenic drive in northwestern New Mexico—and you'll find a few interesting stops along the way.

The recently designated **El Malpais National Monument and Conservation Area** encompasses more than 590 square miles of lava flows and caves, volcanoes, sandstone canyons, and forests centered between Highway 53 and Highway 117 south of Grants. Although some of the natural sites are accessible to passenger cars traveling along the two highways, El Malpais (roughly "The Badlands" in Spanish) is heaven to hikers and backpackers.

Because development so far has been minimal, visitors should check with the El Malpais Information Center at 620 East Santa Fe Avenue (505–285–5406) in Grants before venturing too far off the highways in search of adventure. A detailed map with descriptions of the major natural sites is available. In addition, schedules are posted showing hikes and other activities organized by the National Park Service, the Bureau of Land Management, and the local support group—Los Amigos del Malpais.

Among the sites accessible along Highway 117 are the

Sandstone Bluffs Overlook (10 miles south of I–40), La Ventana Natural Arch (17 miles south of I–40), and The Narrows (1 mile farther south), where the highway passes through a narrow corridor created when lava flowed near the base of huge sandstone cliffs. Intriguing lava formations are in this area. If you were smart enough to pack a picnic, you'll find a lovely spot for lunch at the south end of The Narrows.

Negotiating with private property owners for the sale of parts of El Malpais has been quite a process, and some agreements have yet to be finalized. As a result, two of the most interesting and accessible features of El Malpais are still privately owned, but you can visit them.

The **Candelaria Ice Cave and Bandera Crater** are located in a parklike setting covered with ponderosa pine, spruce, and piñon trees. You start your trek at the trading post on the property, which was once a summer resort complete with cabins. After paying the fee, you hike ½ mile alongside lava flows until you reach a wooden stairway. The steps lead to Candelaria Ice Cave (named for the present owners of the property), located in part of a collapsed lava tube where the temperature never rises above thirty-one degrees. Though walking into the cave is prohibited (liability, you know), you can get a good view of the greenish ice from the viewing platform.

To see Bandera Crater, brace yourself for a longer and steeper hike—about 1½ miles. The 1,000-foot-deep crater was formed during a volcanic eruption 5,000 years ago. Nature has since transformed the spot into a beautiful crater flecked with hardy ponderosa pines. The breezy coolness of the 8,000-foot altitude makes the ridge of the crater a nice place to relax on a hot summer day.

The entrance to the Candelaria Ice Cave and Bandera Crater is located a little less than 26 miles south of Grants on Highway 53; (505) 783–4303. Hours are 8:00 A.M. to about an hour before sunset, and admission is $5.00 for adults and $2.50 for children, with those under five admitted free. But remember, both the ice cave and the crater are slated to become part of El Malpais and thus will be administered by the National Park Service; accordingly, check at the El Malpais Information Center in Grants before planning a trip.

El Morro National Monument is the nation's oldest

national monument. Also known as Inscription Rock, the monument is an oasis in the middle of nowhere; nevertheless, travelers have been stopping here for centuries to drink from the pool of water at the base of the cliff—and to leave behind a little graffiti. A sporadic account of southwestern history from 1605 through the nineteenth century is recorded on what Spanish conquistadores named El Morro, meaning "The Bluff." The inscriptions etched into the vertical stone surface provide a permanent record of the different cultures that influenced the area over the past 400 years. Fifteen years before the Pilgrims landed at Plymouth Rock, the first Spanish inscription was made by explorer Don Juan de Oñate on April 16, 1605, extolling his discovery of the "Sea of the South," now known as the Gulf of California.

Touching the inscriptions or defacing any surface is strictly forbidden. For those, however, who just can't resist the urge to write in stone after viewing El Morro, the visitor center provides near the parking area a rock on which travelers may etch a word or two.

Much earlier visitors to El Morro left their own graffiti in the form of petroglyphs, or ancient rock drawings. You'll find ruins of ancient pueblos here as well. Dating from the thirteenth century, these have been traced to certain Anasazi peoples (the ancestors of the Zuni Indians) and can be found, largely unexcavated, on the top of El Morro.

You can stay here if you wish, at the monument's nine-site, primitive campground. For those who don't like to rough it, however, check out the Vogt Ranch Bed and Breakfast (see McKinley County entry) on Highway 53, 10 miles west of the El Morro turnoff.

El Morro is located just off Highway 53, 43 miles from Grants; (505) 783–4226. Admission is $1.00 per person, with a maximum charge of $3.00 per carload; children under seventeen and seniors are admitted free. Use of the campground is free but is on a first come, first served basis; water is available May through October. Daily hours are 8:00 A.M.–7:00 P.M. from Memorial Day through Labor Day and 8:00 A.M.–5:00 P.M. the remainder of the year.

San Juan County

Similar to Gallup's role in McKinley County, Farmington serves as the major trading center in San Juan County for the Navajo Nation just west of the city. Though Farmington is near the center of the vast, dry Four Corners (more about this later) region, the city is a virtual oasis and a fisherman's paradise with its three rivers flowing around town—the San Juan, the Animas, and the La Plata. San Juan County is also a great place to get in touch with New Mexico's past by visiting its three significant Anasazi ruins sites.

Chaco Culture National Historical Park (Chaco Canyon, for short) contains the finest example of Anasazi pueblo ruins in New Mexico. It may be the singularly most remote tourist attraction in the state, yet people from all over the world find it every year.

Chaco Canyon emerged as the center of Anasazi life in the early tenth century. (The word *Anasazi,* meaning "Ancient Ones," is the name scientists gave to prehistoric farming peoples of the Four Corners region. They are the ancestors of the present-day Pueblo Indians of New Mexico.) Partly because primitive roads connected Chaco Canyon with outlying Anasazi communities, archaeologists believe Chaco was the "capital" of the Anasazi world. In many ways—in their architecture, community life, and social organization—the Anasazi of Chaco Canyon were far more advanced than any other of the Anasazi peoples of the region.

Though Chaco Canyon has been intensely studied for more than a hundred years and scholars theorize about the people who once lived here, many mysteries remain. One of the most intriguing aspects of Chacoan life is the possible connection with the great civilizations of Mexico, such as the ancient Toltecs. Feathers of macaws and other parrots, copper bells, and seashells, all unknown in this area but common in parts of Mexico, have been found in Chaco Canyon. There are also fascinating connections between architecture and astronomy in the remains of the pueblos in the canyon.

The Anasazi's belief that Chaco Canyon was the center of the earth is a powerful one, and the fact that as many as 5,000 people once lived here in a highly civilized society and then mysteriously disappeared is centermost to the lure of

33

the canyon and its ruins. Although rainfall was adequate during the time the Anasazi inhabited Chaco Canyon, persistent droughts are thought to be the reason they finally abandoned the canyon between 1130 and 1180.

To fully experience the park, set aside an entire day for your visit. Otherwise, a stop at the visitor center and a hike around Pueblo Bonito, the largest and most impressive ruin in the canyon, will provide a good overview of the Chaco mystique. Well-marked trails (keyed in a trail guide to selected stops) lead through the maze of chambers.

The park's visitor center has a fine museum and many books on Chaco culture. It's also the only place in the park with water available. The canyon consists of extremely barren, arid land—especially in the summer—so it's smart to bring your own water supply.

Although there are two main routes to Chaco Canyon—neither paved—the best approach is to turn off Highway 44 onto San Juan County Road 7800 at the outpost community of Nageezi, proceed 11 miles to Highway 57, and continue on Highway 57 for 15 miles to the visitor center. These are 26 miles of washboard-type dirt/gravel roads. Though passenger cars are usually adequate, the roads can be impassable during or after substantial rainfall; accordingly, call ahead to check road conditions. Once you get to the federally maintained park, however, the roads are perfectly paved; (505) 988–6727. Admission is $3.00 per vehicle or $1.00 per person. The park is open daily, 8:00 A.M.–5:00 P.M.

For those who are intrigued by Anasazi ruins but aren't up to a trek to Chaco Canyon, two other sites are closer to Farmington: **Aztec Ruins National Monument** and **Salmon Ruin.** Both are easily accessible on paved roads.

The first thing you'll notice about Aztec Ruins National Monument—especially if you visited Chaco Canyon first—is the abundance of trees and a nearby river. Despite the name, these ruins had nothing to do with the Aztec Indians of central Mexico. In fact, the Aztecs lived hundreds of years after this Anasazi pueblo was abandoned. Early Anglo settlers named the site Aztec because they mistakenly believed the Mexican Indians had built the pueblos.

The monument's amazing number of ruins concentrated in a small area make things convenient for visitors. The site of these ruins contains the only fully restored Great Kiva, an especially sacred ceremonial chamber, in North America. A walk through the kiva is definitely the highlight of the visit.

The visitor center of Aztec Ruins is northwest of the city of Aztec (northeast of Farmington), near the junction of U.S. Highway 550 and Highway 44; (505) 334–6174. The monument is open daily from 8:00 A.M. to 6:30 P.M. Memorial Day through Labor Day and from 8:00 A.M. to 5:00 P.M. the remainder of the year. Admission is $1.00 per person, with those under seventeen and over sixty-one admitted free.

Salmon Ruin, a Chacoan pueblo village once connected to Chaco Canyon by a prehistoric road, is the other major Anasazi ruin area in San Juan County. Though unique itself and the site of the San Juan Archaeological Research Center and Library, this smaller site, if you're "ruined out," may be the one to skip.

Salmon Ruin is on U.S. Highway 64, 2 miles west of the community of Bloomfield; (505) 632–2013. Hours are 9:00 A.M.–5:00 P.M. daily, and admission is $1.00 for adults, 50 cents for children ages six to fifteen, and free for children under six and seniors.

Each summer the city of Farmington hosts the widely acclaimed musical pageant *Anasazi, the Ancient Ones* at the Lions Wilderness Park Amphitheater. Although times and dates change from year to year, performances usually run from about mid-June to September. Call the Farmington Convention & Visitors Bureau (505–326–7602 or 1–800–448–1240) for details.

The **Hogback Trading Post,** on the edge of the Navajo Reservation, is *the* place to purchase authentic Navajo arts and crafts in San Juan County. Established in 1871, the Hogback is the oldest trading post—on or off the reservation—serving the Navajos. (The better-known Hubbell Trading Post at Monument Valley wasn't established until 1876.) The Hogback is now run by Tom Wheeler, the great-grandson of the trading post's founder, Joseph Wheeler. The trading post contains almost 10,000 feet of display space in two levels and specializes in fine Navajo-woven rugs. It's located 15 miles west of Farmington on U.S. Highway 64 in the community of Waterflow. The Hogback is open Monday through Saturday, 8:00 A.M.–5:00 P.M.

One of the most memorable places to visit, purely for its I-stood-on-the-spot value, is the **Four Corners Monument,** northwest of Farmington. The absolute barrenness of the area is remarkable. But you can stand on the spot—the only such spot in the United States—where you will truly be in four states at once: New Mexico, Arizona, Utah, and Colorado. It's amazing how far people will travel out of their way to visit a place that would otherwise hold no appeal whatsoever. Still, it *is* a kick.

To get to Four Corners Monument, take U.S. Highway 64 west of Farmington until it meets with U.S. Highway 160 at Teec Nos Pos. (You're now in Arizona.) Then take U.S. Highway 160 north till it meets with Highway 597. (You're back in New Mexico.) Go left on Highway 597 to the monument. It's always open, and there's no admission charge.

On the way to Four Corners Monument from Farmington— along Highway 64, west of the largest Navajo Nation town of Shiprock—you'll pass within viewing distance one of the most majestic and mysterious rock formations in New Mexico: **Shiprock.** The 1,700-foot peak gets its name from its shape, which, at a distance, resembles a two-masted ship sailing on a sea of desert. Though Shiprock changes its appearance at different times of the day, it's said that it looks most like a ship during a midsummer sunset, occasionally appearing to shimmer and drift on an imaginary ocean. Navajos refer to the immense formation as Tse Bi dahi, which means "The Rock with Wings," and several of their folk myths contain references to it. (No one believes me, but I swear Shiprock switches positions across the horizon as you drive by it.)

Back to civilization, a leisurely walking tour of the **Aztec Historic District** in downtown Aztec offers a great change of pace. Centering on the Aztec Museum, more than seventy-five business and residential buildings, including shops and restaurants, are listed on the National Register of Historic Places. The museum houses a fine collection of early pioneer Americana, plus an old wooden oil drilling rig—a tribute to the lucrative oil and gas industry in San Juan County. The museum is at 124 North Main Avenue; (505) 334-9829. Summer hours are 9:00 A.M.–5:00 P.M. from Monday through Saturday and 1:00 P.M.–4:00 P.M. on Sunday; winter hours are 10:00 A.M.–4:00 P.M. from Monday through Saturday. There's no admission charge.

Off the Beaten Path in North Central New Mexico

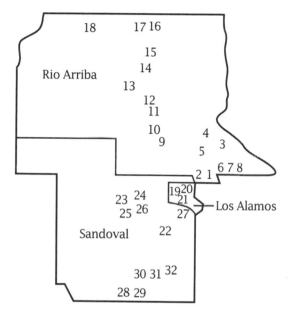

Map showing Rio Arriba, Sandoval, and Los Alamos with numbered locations 1–32.

1. Santa Clara Pueblo
2. Puyé Cliff Dwellings
3. La Chiripada Winery
4. Embudo Station
5. Hacienda de Los Luceros
6. El Santuario de Chimayó
7. Restaurante Rancho de Chimayó
8. Ortega's Weaving Shop
9. Abiquiu
10. Tosh-K-Homa Gallery
11. Ghost Ranch Living Museum
12. The Florence Hawley Ellis Museum of Anthropology
13. Monastery of Christ in the Desert
14. Tierra Wools
15. Casa de Martinez Bed and Breakfast Inn
16. Cumbres & Toltec Scenic Railroad
17. The Jones House
18. Jicarilla Arts and Crafts Museum
19. Bradbury Science Museum
20. Los Alamos Historical Museum
21. Fuller Lodge Art Center and Gallery
22. Dixon Apple Farm
23. Jemez Mountain Inn
24. The Jemez Springs Bath House
25. Los Ojos Restaurant & Saloon
26. Soda Dam
27. Bandelier National Monument
28. Corrales Inn Bed & Breakfast
29. Las Nutrias Winery
30. Prairie Star
31. Coronado State Monument
32. Sandia Man Cave

North Central New Mexico

North central New Mexico is a land of Indian pueblos, forested mountains, hidden hot springs, and magnificent rock formations. The region's beauty so inspired artist Georgia O'Keeffe that she made her home here. In contrast, this region also witnessed the production of the world's first atom bomb.

You'll detect a strong tradition of Hispanic culture and pride in north central New Mexico. The first Spanish colony was established here and some of the state's oldest Hispanic communities continue to thrive in this region. The Hispanic influence lives on in the old Catholic churches, the centuries-old adobe homes, and the high regard for family and quiet respect for "the old ways."

As you set out to explore the intrigue of north central New Mexico, keep in mind that once the sun goes down—even during the summer—it's very cool.

Rio Arriba County

Although situated in one of the most economically depressed areas of the state, Rio Arriba County offers the intrepid traveler a host of adventures if he takes time to search them out. As a bridge between the often-stark landscape of the Four Corners region to its west and the forested, mountainous region to its east, Rio Arriba County is certainly a blending of the two.

In southern Rio Arriba County you'll find the city of Española (partly located in Santa Fe County). Lying near the site of the first Spanish settlement in New Mexico, designated San Juan de los Caballeros in 1598 by Spanish explorer Don Juan de Oñate, Española is a good place to fuel up and start exploring the county.

Just outside Española lies **Santa Clara Pueblo.** The pueblo itself, like most of New Mexico's Rio Grande-area pueblos, is similar to a small rural town and is centered on a mission church and plaza area. Santa Clara is famous for its solid-black pottery, which is prized by collectors. The neatly maintained pueblo is home to many potters and several small galleries. Merrock Galeria (505–753–5602), on the plaza, features the work of Paul Speckled Rock. The multitalented artist channeled his creative energy into other art forms, such as painting, lithography, and sculpture, before venturing into his pueblo's traditional art form in 1983. Although a relative newcomer, Paul has amassed many awards for his works in clay.

From Española take Highway 30 south (on the west side of the Rio Grande) 1³⁄₁₀ miles. The well-marked pueblo entrance is on the left; (505) 753–7326.

Also on the Santa Clara Reservation but 10 miles west of the pueblo you'll find the **Puyé Cliff Dwellings,** in the Santa Clara Canyon Recreational Area. The drive into the canyon is incredibly scenic as you slowly descend among stands of evergreens into the lush, parklike canyon. Though fishing and camping are allowed, for a fee, the highlight is Puyé, which means "Pueblo Ruin Where the Rabbits Assemble" in Tewa, the native Santa Clara Indian language.

As a Registered National Historic Landmark, the dwellings offer adventure to the southwestern history buff who likes a good hike. The earlier dwellings here were caves hollowed in the cliffs; later, adobe structures were built along the slopes and top of the mesa. The Anasazi Indians first settled in the Puyé area in the twelfth century and finally abandoned the area around 1580, probably because of continuing drought.

You can explore the dwellings on two different walking tours. The cliff trail begins at the visitor center and leads up semisteep trails and ladders, going past many of the ancient dwellings built into the cliffs. Stairways link the two levels of cliff dwellings to the mesa top and its large "Community House." For those who prefer a less strenuous course, take the short drive to the mesa-top ruins. Here you can view the 740-room pueblo ruin and its restored ceremonial chamber. Bring a picnic to enjoy the incredible view from this vantage point.

Like exploring many ruins in New Mexico, visiting Puyé can be physically taxing—wear good non-slip shoes or sneakers. Puyé Cliff Dwellings are located off Highway 602 via Highway 30 from Española; (505) 753–7326. Fees are the same for guided or self-guided tours: adults, $4.00; children (ages seven to fourteen) and seniors, $3.00.

While northern New Mexico claims several very good wineries, **La Chiripada Winery** is particularly worth seeking out. Situated among the apple orchards in the small community of Dixon, La Chiripada's tasting room is housed in a whitewashed adobe surrounded by colorful gardens and vineyards. Besides its selection of wines with their Mimbres Indian design labels, the tasting room also sells contemporary pottery. Brothers Michael and Patrick Johnson planted their ten acres of grapes in 1977 and opened the winery on the banks of the Rio Embudo four years later. La Chiripada (meaning "A Stroke of Luck") gets half its grapes from its own vineyards and the remainder from other New Mexico growers.

La Chiripada is on Highway 75 in Dixon; (505) 579–4675. Tasting room hours are 10:00 A.M.–5:00 P.M. Monday through Saturday.

Embudo Station, a historic, 1880s narrow-gauge railroad station between Santa Fe and Taos, is now a casual restaurant on the banks of the Rio Grande. Embudo Station has an outdoor area for patio dining, as well as a country smokehouse shop featuring trout, cheese, and various meats. The restaurant serves barbecued ribs and brisket, ham, turkey, trout, and catfish. Even if you're not hungry, Embudo Station is still a pleasant place to enjoy an appetizer and a beer or a glass of La Chiripada wine while sitting outdoors under the huge cottonwoods. Embudo Station also offers float trips on the Rio Grande in contrast to the white-water experience farther north near Taos. The water is much calmer on this stretch.

The restaurant and float headquarters are located on Highway 68 about 17 miles north of Española; (505) 852–4707. Hours are 12:00 noon–4:00 P.M. Tuesday through Thursday and 12:00 noon–8:00 P.M. Friday through Sunday; however, the restaurant closes mid-November to mid-February.

In 1988 the newly created nonprofit American Studies Foundation purchased a wonderfully secluded Spanish colonial hacienda, **Hacienda de Los Luceros.** The foundation's mission is to study and preserve the rich southwestern tricultural (Native American, Hispanic, and Anglo) heritage of the area, in part by restoring the buildings on the grounds, some of which date from the seventeenth century.

The foundation operates two small restored houses as the Bed and Breakfast at Hacienda de Los Luceros. The Victorian adobe cottage has a pair of one-bedroom suites an dining room, kitchen, and patio ($65 per night ... . $130 for the whole house). The pueblo-style guest house has one bedroom, a bath, a kitchen, and a living room with a kiva fireplace ($75 per night). The foundation also runs a gallery of regional arts in this wooded, pastoral setting. It's open on Saturday and Sunday afternoons and by appointment.

Hacienda de Los Luceros hosts work-study programs in various categories, ranging from hands-on seminars conducted by master artists and craftspersons of the region to archaeological studies emphasizing historic sites. The main house, which was the Spanish colonial headquarters for the region during the 1600s, later served as the courthouse and jail of Rio Arriba County and, from 1921 to 1957, was one of the homes of noted patron of the arts Mary Cabot Wheelwright.

The hacienda is just west of Highway 68, between Embudo and Española, in the tiny community of Los Luceros; (505) 852–4717.

Just inside Rio Arriba County near its border with Santa Fe County, the village of Chimayó lies on the High Road to Taos, that romantic-sounding name for the scenic-though-less-than-direct path connecting Santa Fe to Taos. The old Spanish community of Chimayó is the most interesting stop on the High Road and boasts several "must sees."

The first place to stop is **El Santuario de Chimayó,** known as "Little Lourdes" because of its reputation of miraculous healing and cures similar to those of the famous site in France. Built in 1816, the adobe chapel is widely known as the destination of an annual Holy Week pilgrimage during which thousands walk from all over New Mexico, neighboring states, and even Mexico. Nonetheless, people visit the *santuario* all year long.

The chapel's intricately carved and colorful altar spotlights a 6-foot crucifix, while scores of votive candles maintain a glow nearby. Two side rooms are attached to the chapel. The larger space is devoted to holding the various offerings made over the years, such as small statues, paintings, personal messages of thanks, and photographs. The walls of this room are also lined with the crutches of those who have been cured at Chimayó. The smaller chamber shelters the hole in the floor that contains the sacred, healing dirt (visitors are welcome to take small amounts with them).

Chimayó is accessible from U.S. Highway 285 north of Santa Fe via Highway 503 and then Highway 520. The *santuario* is located on the right, just as you enter the village of Chimayó on Highway 520; (505) 351–4360 (parish office). Services are still held in Santuario de Chimayó, and it's open to the public daily, from the 7:00 A.M. mass to 4:30 or 5:30 P.M., depending on whether any visitors are still in the chapel.

Less than ½ mile farther on Highway 520, you'll see the **Restaurante Rancho de Chimayó** on your right and the Hacienda Rancho de Chimayó (a bed-and-breakfast inn) on your left. If you want a romantic hideaway, stay at the hacienda. If you're hungry, visit the restaurant—and even if you're not hungry, go anyway to enjoy the surroundings.

The restaurant is the former home of Hermenegildo and Trinidad Jaramillo and has been open since 1965. The hundred-year-old adobe provides an intimate dining experience in several small rooms inside and a delightful openness on the terraced patios outside. During spring and summer, colorful flowers and warm temperatures make outside dining the obvious choice. Native New Mexican foods are prepared according to traditional family recipes that stress locally grown products, including the peerless Chimayó red chile. The restaurant has a full bar and carries many Mexican beers, but the house specialty is the potent Chimayó Cocktail. A waitress revealed the recipe as tequila, apple juice, triple sec, creme de cassis, and a dash of lime. The proportions are a secret, but the apple-juice ice cubes and apple-slice garnish make it a perfect before-dinner drink.

The family home of Epifanio and Adelaida Jaramillo became Hacienda Rancho de Chimayó in 1984, after the traditional adobe had been renovated into seven guest rooms filled with turn-of-the-century antiques. Each room has a private bath and sitting area and opens onto an enclosed courtyard. Every morning, your hosts serve a Continental breakfast featuring pastries, fruit, fresh-squeezed orange juice, and coffee or tea.

The restaurant is open daily from 12:00 noon–10:00 P.M. Memorial Day through Labor Day, and Tuesday through Sunday from 12:00 noon–9:00 P.M. the remainder of the year, with the exception of January, when it is closed; (505) 351–4444.

The inn, whose room rates range from $49 to $76, also closes for a few weeks in January; (505) 351-2222.

Continuing on Highway 520 to its junction with Highway 76, you'll come across **Ortega's Weaving Shop** (505-351-4215) and Galeria Ortega (505-351-2288). No matter what time of year you visit, these two neighboring stores are the perfect places to do your Christmas shopping. Eight generations of masterful weaving by the Ortega family is evident in the fine wool rugs, coats, and other outerwear for sale at the weaving shop. You can even watch weavers hand-loom rugs in a room just off the sales area. In addition, the shop has a great selection of Santa Clara Pueblo pottery and books on the Southwest. It's also the place to stock up on dried Chimayó red chile.

Galeria Ortega markets contemporary New Mexican art forms. Wood carvings are featured, including a variety of *bultos,* or representations of saints crafted out of pine or cottonwood limbs. Made by *santeros,* these carvings are uniquely local in appearance. There's also a fine collection of pottery, hand-painted shirts, and handcrafted Nambé ware (bowls, platters, candle holders, etc. that are made from a secret, shiny alloy—named after Nambé Pueblo).

Ortega's Weaving Shop is open Monday through Saturday, 8:30 A.M.–5:30 p.m; Galeria Ortega is open Monday through Saturday, 9:00 A.M.–5:00 P.M., and Sunday, 11:00 A.M.–5:00 P.M. The *galeria* closes on Sundays, however, from mid-November to mid-January.

The village of **Abiquiu** is known for its most famous resident, artist Georgia O'Keeffe, and for the stunning landscape that inspired her, which she referred to as the Faraway. Although O'Keeffe died in 1986 at the age of ninety-eight, people still come from all over to look at the massive adobe walls that guard her still-off-limits home. Her estate may donate the home to the state, which would then turn it into a museum, or so goes the speculation. But for now, you'll have to be satisfied with a glimpse of the outside.

Within sight of O'Keeffe's home you'll find **Tosh-K-Homa Gallery,** which means "Home of the Red Warrior" in Choctaw (not a New Mexico Indian tribe), according to gallery co-owner Le Anatah, who is half-Choctaw herself. The small gallery is as interesting outside as it is inside. During the summer and early fall, the overgrown garden areas are visually stimulating, with huge sunflowers and morning glories mixed in with corn and zucchini. Le Anatah, an artist specializing in historical scenes and a sometime movie extra, and her husband Tex, a Buffalo Bill impersonator who restores and builds saddles, run the gallery, which displays both her paintings and his saddles.

Tosh-K-Homa is just off U.S. Highway 84 at Abiquiu. There's no phone, but you can write P.O. Box 179, Abiquiu, N.M. 87510. The gallery is open daily, except Monday, from 9:00 A.M.–6:00 P.M.

Ghost Ranch Living Museum is a good place to view some of the wildlife found in northern New Mexico. The museum's residents, which include eagles, bears, and elk, were either injured or orphaned before they were brought to the facility, which is managed by the U.S Forest Service. In addition to the wildlife exhibits, other outdoor interpretive programs include a replica of a forest ranger lookout tower complete with fire-fighting information and the "Up through the Ages" exhibit. Here, visitors can gaze through scopes— which have been distributed along a stair-step railing—at the distant multicolored cliffs. For every step up you take, you'll be viewing a "younger" geologic period, as evidenced by the layers of fossilized sediment.

Aquatic environments are also featured. A trout-stocked stream flows throughout the wooded forest reenactment, and an indoor-outdoor beaver enclave called Beaver National Forest celebrates these masters of conservation. Because of these exhibits and many others, the museum is a great educational outing for the kids, but grown-ups also may learn a thing or two about the fragility of our natural environment.

The museum is located on U.S. Highway 84 just north of Abiquiu; (505) 685–4312. It's open daily, except for Mondays in December and January. Summer hours are 8:00 A.M.–6:00 P.M., and winter hours (Labor Day through Easter Sunday) are 8:00 A.M.–4:30 P.M. Admission is a $2.00 donation for adults, $1.00 donation for students and seniors, and free for children under twelve.

Near Ghost Ranch Living Museum off of U.S. Highway 84, you'll find the Ghost Ranch Conference Center (505– 685–4333), which contains two fine museums: **The Florence Hawley Ellis Museum of Anthropology** and The

Ruth Hall Museum of Paleontology. The entire 21,000 acres that constitute what used to be the working Ghost Ranch were donated to the Presbyterian Church (U.S.A.) in 1955. (The ranch got its name from the *brujas,* or witches which were said to haunt the canyons on the ranch.) The conference center serves as a national adult study center and as a steward of the northern New Mexico environment. The anthropology museum centers on past and present peoples who lived within a 60-mile radius of the ranch over a span of 12,000 years, while the paleontology museum's focus is fossils, specifically the study of *Coelophysis,* a type of dinosaur whose mass burial site was discovered here in 1947.

Summer hours (April through September) for both museums are Tuesday through Saturday, 9:00 A.M.–12:00 noon and 1:00–5:00 P.M., and Sunday and Monday, 1:00–5:00 P.M. Winter hours are the same, except that the museums are closed on Monday and are also closed the month of December. There are no admission charges.

The first thing you'll notice after arriving at **Monastery of Christ in the Desert** is the quiet. Getting there is another story. The monastery lies in an isolated but dramatically beautiful canyon along the Chama River, about 27 miles north of Abiquiu, and is surrounded by miles of national forest land. Though the monastery was founded in June 1964 by three monks from New York, the present monastic community began arriving in 1974, seeking the Benedictine life of prayer, reading, studying, and manual labor. If inspiration comes with solitude, then this is the place to get it. Because the monks believe they can best continue the tradition of offering hospitality in the desert by giving their guests an opportunity to share in their way of life, limited accommodations are offered to travelers.

If you're planning an overnight stay, remember that this is not the place to bring a spouse, the kids, or even a friend. It's a place to experience alone. For overnight guests, vegetarian meals are served and library hours are maintained. The serenity of the Chama Canyon wilderness is perfect for escaping daily stresses, meditating, hiking, and just getting back in touch with yourself.

You don't have to stay overnight to experience Christ in the Desert, though. The impressive, contemporary pueblo revival–style chapel and a gift shop are open to nonovernight visitors, while other buildings and the remainder of the grounds are private. The gift shop is filled with books, cards, and other items of a religious nature, but it is unmanned and thus on the honor system. (*Note:* Wearing short pants is unacceptable, and dogs are not welcome.)

The monastery is located off U.S. Highway 84, some 75 miles northwest of Santa Fe. To get there, turn left (north) about ½ mile past Ghost Ranch Living Museum at Forest Service Road Marker 151. Most of the 13-mile drive is not paved but is usually passible in passenger cars; however, during the winter and spring a four-wheel-drive vehicle may be needed. Chapel and gift shop hours are 8:00 A.M.–5:00 P.M. daily. There is no phone (the nearest one is 15 miles away). Write to Guestmaster, Monastery of Christ in the Desert, Abiquiu, N.M. 87510; allow several weeks for correspondence before your overnight visit. While there is no fixed fee to stay in the guest house, $20 per person per day covers monastery expenses.

Continuing north on U.S. Highway 84 brings you to Tierra Amarilla ("Yellow Earth"), the county seat of Rio Arriba County and the place named for the peculiar dirt found in the area. The adjacent village of Los Ojos offers visitors a glimpse at the rich wool-raising and weaving tradition of the area in the form of the **Tierra Wools** store. The shop showcases hand-spun and -dyed yarn, along with handwoven rugs, pillows, jackets, and other items. You'll usually find artisans at work in the back "loom room"—you're welcome to watch. The walls of the store are lined with thousands of multicolored skeins of yarn and rugs that set off the natural beauty of the timeworn wood-planked floors. The Tierra Wools cooperative is a program of Ganados del Valle ("Livestock Growers of the Valley"), whose goal is to ensure that weaving, wool growing, and sheepherding continue as a way of life in this remote region of New Mexico.

Tierra Wools' shop is on the main street of the tiny community of Los Ojos, just west of U.S. Highway 84, north of Tierra Amarilla; (505) 588-7231. From May through October, the shop is open Monday through Saturday from 9:00 A.M. to 6:00 P.M. and Sunday from 11:00 A.M. to 5:00 P.M.; the rest of the year it's open Monday through Saturday from 10:00 A.M. to 5:00 P.M.

The neighboring community of Los Brazos welcomes travelers from all over the world with **Casa de Martinez Bed and Breakfast Inn.** Following the custom of *nuestra casa es su casa* ("our house is your house"), Clarinda Martinez de Sanchez and her husband have offered their family home to the leisurely traveler since 1988.

Although the inn is worlds away from the harshness of urban life, it's a wonderful base from which to explore Santa Fe, Taos, and the Anasazi ruins of northwestern New Mexico—all without packing up and moving each day. Gazing out of the comfortable guest rooms at the distant, pine-covered San Juan Mountains and enjoying Clarinda's home-cooked breakfasts are the real treats of a stay at the inn, originally built in the 1860s by Clarinda's great-grandfather. Although an addition was made to the home after the turn of the century, the thick adobe walls and vigas (ceiling beams made out of logs) are the real thing.

Casa de Martinez is located on the loop that is Los Brazos, off U.S. Highway 84 north of Los Ojos; (505) 558–7858. Daily rates range from $43 to $63. The inn is open from the second weekend in February to the third weekend in October, or thereabouts.

Your trek up U.S. Highway 84 ends in Chama, less than 10 miles from the Colorado border. Chama is a popular spot for sportsmen. The area offers big-game hunting, fishing in the Chama River and nearby Heron and El Vado reservoirs, and some of the West's best and most consistent cross-country skiing in the winter. The town's also a popular place for the nonsporting set because it's the New Mexican home of the **Cumbres & Toltec Scenic Railroad**, North America's longest and highest narrow-gauge steam railroad. The railroad, which connects Chama with Antonito, Colorado, is on the National Historic Register and is owned by the states of both New Mexico and Colorado.

The railroad offers one-way and round-trip excursions (to a midway point and back from either Chama or Antonito) from late spring through midfall. The train has fully enclosed and semienclosed cars, all of which provide for unobstructed viewing in comfort during your journey through groves of pine and aspen, striking rock formations, and other breathtaking views. Consider a late September or early October trip

47

Cumbres & Toltec Scenic Railroad

so as to miss the crowds and catch the aspens at their golden best. Also note that all the trips take the better part of a day (10:30 a.m–4:30 P.M., 10:00 A.M.–5:00 P.M., etc.), and although summer is usually warm and pleasant it's best to be prepared for cooler weather by wearing long pants and bringing a light jacket.

The 64 miles of railroad are the finest remaining example of a vast network that once connected commercial outposts in the Rocky Mountain region. Spiked down in 1880 as the

San Juan Extension of the Denver & Rio Grande Railroad, the Cumbres & Toltec was built to serve the rich mining camps in the mountains.

The Chama depot is on Terrace Street downtown; (505) 756–2151. Though tickets may be available for purchase at the depot, it's best to make reservations as far in advance as possible. The railroad has several ride options daily from late May through mid-October. Fares range from $29.00 to $43.50 for adults and $11.00 to $21.00 for children under twelve.

Down the street from the depot you'll find **The Jones House,** a restored two-story home built in 1928 that is now operated as a bed-and-breakfast by Sara and Philip Cole. The seemingly contradictory adobe building material coupled with its Tudor design makes an interesting and attractive home.

Chama was a boomtown and important railroad center at the time W. O. Evans opened Chama's first bank and had this home built for him. The home was then bought by Mr. Jones in 1943 and served as a residence until the Coles purchased it in 1987. An ample selection of books, magazines, and board games are available to guests in the well-lighted sitting area. Because of Philip's fascination with trains and the railroad, you'll also find choice railroad reading while you occasionally peer out the window at the Cumbres & Toltec railroad station and yard down the street.

The inn is at the corner of Terrace and Third in downtown Chama; (505) 756–2908. Rates range from $45 to $55.

Heading west out of Chama on U.S. Highway 84 (it will meet U.S. Highway 64 about 15 miles west—continue on U.S. 64, for otherwise you'll end up in Pagosa Springs, Colorado), you'll drive through parts of the vast Jicarilla Apache Reservation and into the community of Dulce, the headquarters of the Indian reservation. Unlike New Mexico's Pueblo Indians, ancestors of the Jicarilla Apache were nomadic—their life-style was determined by the seasons and migration of wildlife. They traveled throughout southern Colorado, northeastern New Mexico, and the panhandles of Texas and Oklahoma. The reservation was established in 1887.

To learn more about the Jicarilla Apache, visit the **Jicarilla Arts and Crafts Museum** (505–759–3242, ext. 274), housed in a modest green building on U.S. Highway 64 (Jicarilla Boulevard) in Dulce. The museum is open daily, 7:00 A.M.–

5:00 P.M.; there's no admission charge. The reservation will also issue permits for camping, hunting, and fishing. Call (505) 759–3255 for any information regarding the Jicarilla Apache. For thoroughly modern lodging, the Best Western Jicarilla Inn is the place to stay. It's located on U.S. Highway 64; (505) 759–3663.

During your visit—or on your way from Chama to Dulce— check out the Broken Butt Saloon (the butt of a gun, that is) to experience its Old West atmosphere and dances on weekends. The Broken Butt is in the middle of nowhere, fifteen minutes east of Dulce at the junction of U.S. Highway 64 and U.S. Highway 84; (505) 756–2381. Hours vary.

Los Alamos County

A small city on the Pajarito Plateau, Los Alamos was once home only to a handful of ranchers and to a school for boys. But world events in the 1940s have forever made Los Alamos a household name.

Los Alamos, county seat of New Mexico's smallest county of the same name, has a fascinating history because of the role it played in the top-secret Project Y (a.k.a. the Manhattan Project)—the development of the world's first atom bomb— during World War II. For historical reasons alone Los Alamos is an interesting place to visit, but the community also happens to be set in one of New Mexico's most beautiful sites—a military requirement, along with its remoteness, to keep the scientists content during the long ordeal.

A thirty-minute drive from Santa Fe, Los Alamos today is quite a normal town, despite its famous past. Originally named Otowi, the town got its new name from the Los Alamos Ranch School, founded in 1917 by Ashley Pond, Jr., as a place where frail boys (from wealthy families, usually back East) could grow into robust men. The school closed in 1943 after the government chose isolated Otowi as the site for the monumental Manhattan Project.

In some ways Los Alamos has the feel of a "company town" because Los Alamos National Laboratory, technological successor to the Manhattan Project days, is by far the community's largest employer, providing thousands of jobs.

Operated by the University of California for the U.S. Department of Energy, the lab itself contains the most interesting attraction of all in Los Alamos: the **Bradbury Science Museum.**

The extensive museum chronicles the dawning of the atomic age by focusing on achievements in weapons development, alternate energy sources, and biomedical research. Additional exhibits feature the lab's ongoing work in such areas as computer technology, nuclear safeguards, and basic research exploring the nature of nuclei, atoms, and molecules. Photographs, documents, and newspaper headlines provide a timeline of significant world events covering the early 1930s to the mid-1960s.

Throughout the day, the museum's theater presents a twenty-minute film called *The City That Never Was,* which traces Los Alamos's history with actual period film footage and reenactments of notable events in the city's past. The film is a nice break from the rest of the large, info-packed museum, which can be a little overwhelming if you try to absorb everything.

The exhibits, however, are very well presented, employing lots of interactive video screens to make things a little more accessible and comfortable to nontechies. More than thirty-five hands-on exhibits invite visitor participation: You can align a laser, pinch plasma, and monitor radiation. Plan to stay at least two hours if you want a good overview of everything—and longer if you want to experience the exhibits in depth.

The museum is located on the grounds of the lab, Building 200 in Tech Area 3 on Diamond Drive (follow the signs to the well-marked museum); (505) 667–4444. It's open Tuesday through Friday, 9:00 A.M.–5:00 P.M., and Saturday through Monday, 1:00–5:00 P.M. There's no admission charge.

While the Bradbury Science Museum is high-tech and scientific, the **Los Alamos Historical Museum** is a little more low-key and personal. It traces the area's history beyond its military role, although the war years get big play here also. The small stone-and-log museum, the former infirmary and guest house of the Los Alamos Ranch School—preserves artifacts from Los Alamos's past, including a geology exhibit and household items common during the war years. It also has a well-stocked bookstore.

The Los Alamos Historical Museum is at 1921 Juniper on the grounds of the Fuller Lodge Cultural Center; (505) 662-6272. Hours are 10:00 A.M.–4:00 P.M. from Monday through Saturday and 1:00–4:00 P.M. on Sunday. There is no admission charge.

At one time, Fuller Lodge provided the first housing for the Manhattan Project scientists, before the establishment was turned into a hotel and restaurant. Today it's the Fuller Lodge Cultural Center, a multipurpose community center that houses the **Fuller Lodge Art Center and Gallery**. The art center features the works of regional artists in its permanent collection, together with collections on loan from Los Alamos citizens, as well as traveling exhibits. Many items are for sale to the public. The art center also sponsors various classes, lectures, and shows throughout the year.

The art center is on the second floor of the Fuller Lodge Cultural Center (though it has its own entrance), at 2123 Central Avenue; (505) 662–9331. Gallery hours are 10:00 A.M.–4:00 P.M. Monday through Saturday and 1:00–4:00 P.M. on Sunday.

Sandoval County

Although Sandoval County has led New Mexico in population growth during the past five years and is projected to continue as the fastest-growing county until the turn of the century, its growth is due to the population explosion of one city—Rio Rancho, a boomtown bedroom community of Albuquerque. Rio Rancho is, however, very atypical of the rest of the county. The remainder of Sandoval County is pleasantly rural, containing rock formations, forests, mountains, and Indian Pueblos.

Southern Sandoval County would normally be considered more "central" than "north central" New Mexico, but because this book is divided by county, it'll be classified as the latter. The region, however, will be divided into southern and northern Sandoval County.

Northern Sandoval County

Beyond Cochiti Lake and nearby Cochiti Pueblo you'll find **Dixon Apple Farm.** Visitors are welcome to the quaint orchard at the base of the Cañada Valley's crimson cliffs all year, but it's the few weeks in middle to late September and early October that make this place special to those who partake in the annual fall pilgrimage, mostly Albuquerqueans, in search of Dixon's patented and prized Champagne apple. Along with the Champagne, the farm grows and sells Double Red Delicious during opening weekend; a few weeks later Dixon's other patented apple, Sparkling Burgundy, arrives, as does the popular Rome.

Off the salesroom you can watch the apples being washed, sorted, and packed. Only flawless ones make it to the salesroom, the rest are destined to become cider for those who want their apples without the crunch.

A tiny, rapidly flowing brook runs through the farm, adding even more to the valley's allure. A scattering of picnic tables is available for those wanting to linger awhile. Take a wedge of sharp cheddar to have with a crisp Champagne along the brook for your own little bit of heaven.

There's no set date when apple season begins at Dixon—fine apple growing is an art as well as a science, you know—so if you don't want to be left out, start calling (505) 465–2976 in mid-September. During season, hours are 8:00 A.M.–5:00 P.M. daily.

To get to Dixon's, take the Cochiti Lake exit off I–25, about 28 miles north of Albuquerque. Go left, toward Cochiti, about 18½ miles (the last 2 of which are gravel) to get to the orchards.

The Jemez Mountains, particularly the Jemez Springs area, are a favorite with hiking, camping, and cross-country-skiing devotees. Named for the many hot springs hidden in the area, the village of Jemez Springs provides the perfect getaway weekend for weary city folks.

Let the **Jemez Mountain Inn** be your base for the weekend. The main part of the inn has been the center of activity in the area for more than a hundred years, serving as the town silver assayer's office and barbershop, among other things. The building assumed its role as the Amber Lodge in 1936 until Captain Bill and Sharon Young purchased the property in 1989, when they passed through Jemez Springs on a motorcycle and noticed the inn was for sale.

Bill says all the rooms are different and each has a story. He even claims that mobsters from the East Coast laid low here in the 1930s. In addition to running the inn, Bill also coordinates a program called Pueblo Mariners of New Mexico, in which he arranges ocean voyages for Indian youth—which idea is interesting in itself, given that New Mexico is composed of desert and mountains, with no ocean for hundreds of miles.

Like nearly everything else in Jemez Springs, the Jemez Mountain Inn is on the main drag (Highway 4), within walking distance of other places and attractions; (505) 829–3926. Rates range from $25 to $40.

The Jemez Springs Bath House has also been around for more than 100 years, having originally been built by the Jemez Indians to utilize the curative waters that bubble from the ground along the Jemez River. Now owned by the town and leased out, the bathhouse is bare-bones and basic, qualities that add to its peculiar attraction.

Separate women's and men's wings each have four smooth, concrete tubs that are meticulously scrubbed after every use, even though they may not look like it because of the high mineral buildup over time. In addition to mineral soaks, which are said to relax muscles and heal sore joints, the bathhouse offers sweat wraps and massages.

Thirty-minute baths run $5.00 ($2.00 extra for the sweat wrap), and massages are $14.00 for thirty minutes and $24.00 per hour. The Jemez Springs Bath House is on Highway 4 in Jemez Springs; (505) 829–3303.

If you like your soaks au naturel, head to the pools of Spence Hot Springs. The pools are the more accessible springs in the mountainous area under U.S. Forest Service jurisdiction. The forest service warns though, "Don't drink or snort the water up your nose, because some hot springs in the area may contain an amoeba called Naegleri Fowlerii which can cause a fatal brain infection called PAM, Primary Amoebic Meningoencephalitis. Though deaths are rare, keep your head above water just in case."

Spence Hot Springs are in the vicinity of mile markers 24 and 25 on Highway 4, 7 miles north of the Jemez Springs Bath House, on the right side of the road. You'll see a crude parking area and a sign that says NO PARKING AFTER 10 P.M. (There used to be a Spence Hot Springs sign, but apparently every time one was put up someone stole it.) Then follow the prim-

itive path a little less than 1 mile up the hill. The
admission charges or designated hours, but it's a
you shouldn't be there after 10 P.M.

For a beer and burger after your soak, check out **Los Ojos
Restaurant & Saloon,** across Highway 4 from the Jemez
Mountain Inn (505-829-3547). It's been around since 1947.
LOS OJOS IS HOME OF THE FAMOUS JEMEZ BURGER—ONE JELLUVA
JAMBURGER, as its sign proclaims. (At the very least, the sign
makes it clear how to pronounce Jemez: rhymes with
"famous.") You can even play a game of pool while you wait
for your Jamburger.

For those of you who must include something educational
when you travel, don't miss the Jemez State Monument, 1
mile north of Jemez Springs on, what else, Highway 4; (505)
829-3530. The monument preserves the ruins of both the
old village of Guisewa, built approximately 600 years ago by
the ancestors of the nearby Jemez Pueblo Indians, and of the
mission church of San Jose de los Jemez, built by Spanish
colonists in the early 1620s. The visitor center exhibits interpret the area's history from the perspective of the Jemez
Indians. The monument is open daily from 9:00 A.M. to 6:00
P.M. May 1 through September 15 and from 8:00 A.M. to 5:00
P.M. the rest of the year. Admission is $2.00 for adults and
$1.00 for children ages six to sixteen.

Nearby **Soda Dam** is about ½ mile farther north on Highway 4 from Jemez State Monument. The natural dam on the
Jemez River does not create a lake but, rather, channels the
river through a short tunnel to provide a small waterfall and
pool on the other side—perfect for cooling off in the summer.
(*Note:* The pool's depth is unpredictable because of rocks
often deposited by the river; accordingly, *never* attempt to
dive into the small pool.) During cooler times of the year,
when the summer crowds are gone, sightseers and picnickers
can walk up the trail that snakes to the top of the rock formation and provides a peek at the river on the other side. Eventually, the U.S. Forest Service plans a visitor information
center at Soda Dam.

Bandelier National Monument, in northeast Sandoval
County, is one of the most spectacular places to hike in New
Mexico. It was designated a National Monument in 1916 to
protect one of the largest concentrations of archaeological

To get to the Corrales Inn, go 2⁷⁄₁₀ miles north on Corrales Road from its intersection with Alameda Boulevard; then take a left just past an elementary school. The inn will be on your right; (505) 897–4422. Rates range from $50 to $60.

If you're into wine, stop by **Las Nutrias Winery** while in Corrales. Housed in a seemingly out-of-place 1897 Sears and Roebuck prefab Victorian home, Las Nutrias offers complimentary wine tastings plus tours. You can even relax on the winery's front lawn under huge cottonwoods and enjoy a glass of your recent purchase. Las Nutrias Winery is at 4036 Corrales Road; (505) 897–7863 or 898–5690. It's open Wednesday through Sunday from 12:00 noon to 6:00 P.M. and other times by appointment.

Like Corrales, the town of Bernalillo is another bedroom community of Albuquerque with a rural flavor. Bernalillo lies along I–25 north of Albuquerque and is home to one of the finest restaurants in the Albuquerque metro area—**Prairie Star.** Housed in a large adobe, the restaurant commands a most dramatic view of the Sandia Mountains at sunset, when they turn an intense watermelon red; after dark, the view is replaced by the glittering lights of Albuquerque. Prairie Star's menu is a worthy match for the view. Featuring New American cuisine, the restaurant serves such tempting creations as Avocado Alfredo, Swordfish Waldorf, and Cajun Pork Wellington.

Prairie Star is just off Highway 44 on Jemez Dam Road near Bernalillo; (505) 867–3327. Dinner is served Monday through Thursday from 5:00 to 10:00 P.M. and Friday and Saturday from 5:00 to 11:00 P.M.

The annual New Mexico Wine Festival is held in Bernalillo on Labor Day weekend to celebrate the long wine-making tradition in New Mexico generally and in Bernalillo specifically. Spanish colonists brought grapes along with other reminders of civilization, and the missionaries of the period began making wine for sacramental and personal uses. Eventually Bernalillo became the center of wine production in New Mexico during the eighteenth and nineteenth centuries. The festival includes a juried art show, food booths, entertainment and, of course, winetastings from most of New Mexico's wineries. (See the list of wineries on page 146.)

Coronado State Monument, located near Bernalillo, is popular with Albuquerque visitors because of its proximity to the city. The monument commemorates the 1540 expedition of Francisco Vásquez de Coronado in search of the riches of the legendary Seven Cities of Cibola. Coronado and his soldiers camped near the now-deserted Kuaua Pueblo, the site of the monument. The park contains a trail through the pueblo ruins, which includes a reconstructed kiva (or ceremonial chamber). The visitor center contains exhibits on the history of the Rio Grande Valley. You can even try on an armored conquistador outfit complete with headgear, just like Coronado wore.

The monument is located 1 mile northwest of Bernalillo on Highway 44; (505) 867–5351. It's open daily from 9:00 A.M. to 6:00 P.M. April through September 15 and from 8:00 A.M. to 5:00 P.M. the rest of the year. Admission is $2.00 for those over fifteen.

The small community of Placitas lies east of Bernalillo, across I–25 in the foothills of the Sandia Mountains. Placitas was a popular place for communes in the late 1960s and is now a popular place for pricey new homes in the rambling adobe tradition, though old adobes still exist near the community's center. An interesting site near Placitas in Las Huertas Canyon is the **Sandia Man Cave,** where artifacts of Sandia Man (prehistoric peoples of the area) were excavated by University of New Mexico archaeologists in the late 1930s.

Though it's too dark to really see, the cave doesn't go more than a few feet before becoming a narrow tunnel that reaches back 300 feet. It's thus not truly possible to venture more than a few feet into the cave, and indeed trying to do so may be dangerous even with a flashlight; nevertheless, the first few feet give a good sense of what life was like for Sandia Man more than 10,000 years ago.

The cave is about 4 miles southeast of Placitas on N.M. 165 (3 of these miles are gravel through Cibola National Forest). You'll see a sign marking the parking area at the start of the ½-mile trail to the steps at the cave's entrance.

Off the Beaten Path in the Santa Fe and Taos Region

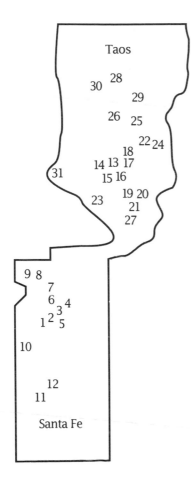

1. Canyon Road
2. Morning Star Gallery
3. El Farol
4. Tengam's Sanctuary & Garden of Atomic Art
5. International Museum of Folk Art
6. The Bishop's Lodge
7. Shidoni
8. San Ildefonso Pueblo
9. Cottonwood Trading Post
10. El Rancho de las Golondrinas
11. Madrid
12. Mine Shaft Tavern
13. Kit Carson Home
14. Martinez Hacienda
15. The Blumenschein Home
16. The Harwood Foundation Museum
17. Taos Inn
18. Bed & Breakfast at the Mabel Dodge Luhan House
19. San Francisco de Asis Church
20. Don Pascual Martinez Bed & Breakfast
21. Whistling Waters
22. Taos Pueblo
23. Picuris Pueblo
24. Overland Sheepskin Company
25. Millicent Rogers Museum
26. Rio Grande Gorge Bridge
27. Fort Burgwin
28. Red River State Trout Hatchery
29. Taos Ski Valley
30. Wild Rivers Recreation Area
31. Ojo Caliente Mineral Springs

Santa Fe and Taos Region

The counties that boast the art meccas of Santa Fe and Taos have more to offer the traveler than what's confined inside these cities' boundaries. But, oh what those city limits enclose! When people daydream about New Mexico, they're most likely to conjure up images of the historic districts of Santa Fe and Taos: the narrow streets, the richly textured curves of adobe walls, the quaint shops, hidden cafes, and ever present art galleries—all set against glorious tree-covered mountains.

But in this region, beyond the city limits, you'll discover New Mexico's highest mountain and wildest river. You'll also find Indian pueblos, first-class downhill and cross-county skiing, historic museums, a revived ghost town, and a mineral springs resort. But most of all you'll encounter awesome scenery and flawless weather no matter what time of year you visit.

Santa Fe County

It's a city, it's a style, it's even a cologne and a cookie (by Pepperidge Farms). It's Santa Fe, of course, and it's New Mexico's own. Set against the breathtaking Sangre de Cristo ("Blood of Christ") Mountains, the city of Santa Fe, aptly located in Santa Fe County, is a city of superlatives built around a historic plaza: It's the nation's oldest capital (founded in 1610), it's also the nation's highest capital, at 7,000 feet; and it boasts the country's oldest church (San Miguel Chapel) as well as oldest public building (Palace of the Governors, now a museum).

Despite its fame or, rather, because of it—Santa Fe presents a major dilemma when writing a book such as this. Writing only one chapter in a guidebook—albeit a selective guide—on Santa Fe is a little like being asked to explain nuclear physics in a hundred words or less. It's a little overwhelming. Add to that the rest of Santa Fe County and it gets more than a little overwhelming. Santa Fe is certainly the most-written-about city in New Mexico, and its paths have been so well beaten by visitors from all over the globe that it hardly seems anything new could be written about "The City Different" in a travel book. Acknowledging that fact, this chapter will first advise you on experiencing the city's historic/shopping district without directing you to particular spots; it will then cover a few places outside the inner core, before moving on to concentrate on those places in Santa Fe County but outside the city.

It's hard not to fall in love with Santa Fe. The city oozes quaintness, uniqueness, and all those other "nesses" that have made it New Mexico's most popular visitor destination for decades. If ever there was a New Mexico city perfect for exploring on foot, Santa Fe would be it. Several museums and countless galleries, shops, cafes, and historic sites are within easy walking distance from the Santa Fe Plaza. Surprises lurk around every corner. To advise visitors on what to see here is pointless and would undermine the sense of self-discovery that Santa Fe is all about. This is not a cop-out on the part of a lazy travel writer. Trust me.

If you must, go ahead and consult your conventional guidebook on the slickest galleries, the toniest restaurants, and the chicest shops. And then put it away and heed the following advice to "experience" Santa Fe's downtown by yourself or with a friend (avoid going with a group, if it's your first visit).

Take off your watch and take a deep breath. Park near the plaza, if you can find a spot. Then skip the plaza (though you'll probably want to check out the jewelry sold by Native Americans under the Palace of the Governors portal). Head out on any one of the streets and wind around until you think you're a little lost. Relax. Drift around, entering whichever places appeal to you. And don't try to see everything; you'll never have time, even if you stay here for days. Duck into a cafe for a cup of coffee or a glass of wine and rest your feet awhile. Check out the museums and historic churches, if you're so inclined. Time seems to stop when you're in Santa Fe, so above all don't hurry. Just enjoy the sensory pleasures of the city: the smell of burning piñon wafting from the chimneys, the rich textures and curves of adobe and wood, the muted colors of the city set against that intense azure sky. You'll see much more, have more fun, and be less stressed than if you felt you had to see certain places within a specified time frame. Now you're ready to venture out a bit.

To get an idea of Santa Fe's upscale appeal, take a stroll down **Canyon Road,** about 8 blocks southeast of the plaza. As the most coveted address in town, this 2-mile avenue was once part of an Indian trail to the Pecos pueblos and is now synonymous with art and money, though it's remained slightly "beyond the fray" of rampant tourism so as to retain its inherent charms. You'll find many of the city's finer galleries along this narrow promenade, as well as a distinctive medley of restaurants and shops.

Even if you can't afford to purchase anything, one of the more interesting stops along Canyon Road is **Morning Star Gallery.** Though it deals in investment-quality antique American Indian art, Morning Star seems more like a museum that allows visitors to purchase the exhibits. The gallery doesn't limit itself to Indian art from New Mexico, though you'll certainly find plenty of it here. An exquisite Acoma Pueblo pot may go for as much as $4,500, and Navajo blankets from the 1800s reach into the $45,000–$50,000 range. It's incredible to see these items up close and wonder what the potter or weaver would have done with all that money.

Morning Star is located at 513 Canyon Road; (505) 982–8187. It's open Monday through Saturday, 10:00 A.M.– 5:00 P.M.

Following an afternoon of gallery-hopping along Canyon Road, ease into **El Farol** for a taste of the unexpected, and expect to be entertained. This fine restaurant specializes in *tapas* (roughly translated as "appetizers"), a serving style native to Spain, where each selection is presented on its own small plate. Choose several to make a meal from the extensive menu. The *tapas* come hot or cold and run the gamut from meat and chicken to seafood and vegetarian. This is a great way to sample a variety of different foods yet still have a hearty meal. El Farol's bar has live entertainment every night, variously featuring jazz, blues, flamenco, or folk sounds.

El Farol is at 808 Canyon Road; (505) 983–9912. It's open daily for dinner, 6:00–10:00 P.M.; bar hours are 4:00 P.M.–2:00 A.M.

Tengam's Sanctuary & Garden of Atomic Art is the most unusual and uncommercial spot on Canyon Road. It exhibits both indoors and out the striking sculpture of Tony Price. For years, Price collected shiny metal scraps of assorted hardware left over from nuclear weapons production in Los Alamos (see Los Alamos entry). He turned this refuse into remarkably beautiful works of art resembling images from many of the world's religions. His mission was to somehow balance the horror of nuclear weapons with the positive energies of religion to maintain peace.

To fully experience the drama of this place, visit on an overcast, breezy afternoon. The outdoor sculpture garden will eerily come to life as the moving parts of certain works clink, gong, and chime their dissonant, melancholy tones as if warning the world to pay attention to Price's message. It's a chilling experience and perfectly fits the mood of the sanctuary.

Tengam's is at the rear of 403 Canyon Road; (505) 983–1588. It's open weekdays from 10:00 A.M. to 5:00 P.M. and weekends from 1:00 to 5:00 P.M.

In contrast to the museums in downtown Santa Fe, the small cluster of museums off Camino Lejo in southeast Santa Fe have an open, contemporary feel. Alongside the Wheelwright Museum of the American Indian and the Museum of Indian Arts and Culture you'll find the more unusual **International Museum of Folk Art.** Set aside a few hours to soak up the eclectic exhibits of various folk arts from more than a hundred countries.

As the largest museum of its kind in the world, the facility's highlight is the Girard Collection, the lifetime collection of the famous architect Alexander Girard and his wife. The brightly colored displays reflect diverse cultures' special talents at channeling their creativity into toys, textiles, costumes, masks, and more. There are no labels in the Girard Collection wing to interfere with the aesthetics of the exhibits. There is, however, a printed guide whose entries correspond to the numbered exhibits so you can make your excursion as "left brain" as you want.

The Folk Art Museum is at 706 Camino Lejo; (505) 827–8350. Admission is $3.50 for adults, and children under sixteen are admitted free. (*Note:* A two-day pass for all four Santa Fe museums—Museum of New Mexico system only—is available for $6.00.) The museum is open daily, 10:00 A.M.–5:00 P.M., except during January and February, when it's closed on Mondays.

When considering lodging, Santa Fe's outstanding choices include historic downtown hotels, quaint bed-and-breakfasts, and modern resorts. But the one to check out when you're interested in checking in for a while is **The Bishop's Lodge,** just five minutes north of the city in the tranquil Tesuque Valley.

In the 1800s this 1,000-acre ranch was the personal retreat of Father Jean Baptiste Lamy, who became the archbishop of Santa Fe. Father Lamy's story lives on in Willa Cather's book *Death Comes for the Archbishop,* and his chapel still stands just as he left it, as a focal point on the ranch. The historical aspect of the lodge blends well with the modern accommodations and comforts. Its guest rooms are done in classic, Southwestern/Santa Fe style, many with fireplaces and balconies or terraces. As a full-service resort, the lodge allows you to opt out of going into the city for fun every day. There's much to do on the grounds of the lodge itself, and sports enthusiasts will find tennis courts, a skeet- and trap-shooting range, a swimming pool, and horses for riding.

The Bishop's Lodge is located off Bishop's Lodge Road; (505) 983–6377. Rates, without meals, range from $82 to $240, depending on the season and type of room or suite. A modified American Plan, which includes breakfast and dinner, is also available.

An aside is appropriate here: Avoid the city of Santa Fe during summer if you can. Though many businesses depend on this "tourist season," Santa Feans will heartily thank me if any of you heed this advice. And you too will be grateful after you've explored this captivating city without so many people. Avoiding Santa Fe in the summer is, however, impossible if you're a devout opera fan who's always dreamed of attending the world-famous Santa Fe Opera. You guessed it; the opera season runs July through August. Keep in mind, though, that it's not unheard of for tickets to sell out six months in advance. And although there can be crowds in Santa Fe around the Christmas holidays as well, that's just such a magical time to be in Santa Fe that it's hard to tell someone to avoid December too.

The community of Tesuque, named for nearby Tesuque Pueblo, is about 8 miles north of Santa Fe via Highway 590 (or U.S. Highway 84/285 and then Highway 591). This quiet little community has become quite-pricey real estate over the years as Santa Feans and others have come to appreciate the simple tree-covered beauty of this slow-paced valley.

If you're into fine art with a penchant for sculpture, **Shidoni** is the place for you. This intriguing spot is actually three spots: Shidoni Contemporary Gallery, Shidoni Bronze Gallery, and Shidoni Sculpture Garden. Shidoni (the word for a Navajo greeting to a friend) is not only a place for art lovers to visit but also an important resource for artists. Established as a foundry in 1971 by sculptor Tommy Hicks, Shidoni has evolved into an internationally known fine-art casting facility. Bronze pourings are held every Saturday from 12:00 noon to 4:30 P.M., and the public is welcome to watch as 2,000-degree molten bronze is poured into the ceramic shell molds, one of several steps in the casting process.

The sculpture garden is a favorite of many visitors to Shidoni. You're immediately struck that this place is special when you pull into the parking area and are greeted by colorful things springing forth from the earth. As you gaze beyond, you'll notice that there are many more intriguing and sometimes-outlandish works of art positioned among old apple trees in a spacious grassy area. A crisp sunny day is perfect for examining the garden.

Shidoni is 5 miles north of Santa Fe, just south of Tesuque on Bishop's Lodge Road; (505) 988–8001. The galleries and garden are open Monday through Saturday, 9:00 A.M.–5:00 P.M.

If you're hungry after your visit to Shidoni, grab a bite at the Tesuque Village Market (505–988–8848) on Highway 591 in Tesuque. This laid-back restaurant, deli, and wineshop serves up great soups and sandwiches and wine by the glass; the market is also known for its selection of scrumptious desserts. Patio seating, too, is available. The market, a welcome change from some of the stuffier places in the city, is open daily, 7:00 A.M.–9:00 P.M.

While you're in the area, stop at Camel Rock along U.S. Highway 84/285 on Tesuque Pueblo; the site offers a great place to get your picture taken with this striking, and appropriately named rock formation. The rock is fenced off, so you can't sit on its head or anything, but the fence doesn't ruin the photograph—you'll hardly notice it.

Northwest of Santa Fe you'll discover **San Ildefonso Pueblo.** Set in the Rio Grande valley and flanked by vast stands of cottonwoods, the pueblo is a beautifully maintained village laid out in the traditional manner with mission church and plaza. The Jemez Mountains in the distance complete the scene. Similar to Santa Clara Pueblo, San Ildefonso is famous for its matte black-on-black pottery, though other types are also created here. One of New Mexico's most famous Native American artists, the late Maria "Poveka" Martinez, was from San Ildefonso and revived this traditional art form. A museum on the pueblo is dedicated to her.

To get the best feel for the art and the people of New Mexico's northern pueblos all in one place, visit San Ildefonso Pueblo during the Eight Northern Indian Pueblos' Artist & Craftsman Show, held every July. Because this is a popular event, you can expect lots of people; nevertheless, if you're serious about buying Indian art or jewelry directly from Native Americans in a lovely setting, it's worth braving the crowds to attend.

Though San Ildefonso welcomes visitors daily from 8:00 A.M. to 5:00 P.M., you must first register with the visitor center; call ahead for specific dates of events. There's no admission fee, but camera and sketching fees do apply. San Ildefonso is 22 miles northwest of Santa Fe: 16 miles north on U.S. Highway 285/84 and then 6 miles west on Highway 502; (505) 455–2273.

Just west of San Ildefonso Pueblo on Highway 502 you'll come across the **Cottonwood Trading Post** (505–455–7596). This tiny store exists for area pueblo residents and others who live in the vicinity. It not only buys and sells Indian-made pottery, jewelry, and weavings but is also a legitimate trading post complete with groceries and household items. Staff members are extremely knowledgeable about Native American arts because they deal directly with the artists themselves. The trading post is open daily, generally 8:00 A.M.–7:00 P.M.

South of Santa Fe, near the community of La Cienega, you'll find **El Rancho de las Golondrinas** ("The Ranch of the Swallows"). This isolated, 200-acre living history museum is part of one of the most historic ranches in the Southwest. The ranch (of the same name) was founded in the early 1700s as a stopping place on El Camino Real, "The Royal Road" connecting Mexico City to Santa Fe. The museum has as its focus eighteenth-century life on a working Spanish colonial ranch. Every effort has been made to re-create the ranch as it was during this period: Crops are grown, orchards and vineyards are tended to, and sheep, goats, turkeys, geese, and ducks mill about. Though there's a small "traditional" indoor museum on the grounds, the joy of a visit to Las Golondrinas is walking among all the outbuildings and gardens.

Las Golondrinas really comes alive during its spring and fall festivals, especially the latter. Each October you can step back in time to all the sights and smells of an authentic fall harvest from the past. You'll witness costumed interpreters first carding, spinning, and dyeing wool and then weaving it into rugs. You can also see sugarcane becoming molasses with the help of a burro-driven press. Then there are blacksmiths and wheelwrights at work and a wonderful water-driven mill spinning among the golden poplars. And gourds, sunflowers, and red chiles lay drying in the sun, while juice is crushed from freshly picked apples (samples available). The stillness and anticipation of an autumn day in the country creep into your soul and take hold at Las Golondrinas and are well worth the trek.

El Rancho de las Golondrinas is located south of Santa Fe. Take the exit off I–25 at the Downs of Santa Fe and follow the signs; (505) 471–2261. The museum is open June through August, Wednesday through Sunday, 10:00 A.M.–4:00 P.M. Admission is $3.00 for adults, $2.00 for children ages thirteen to eighteen, and $1.00 for children ages five to twelve. Spring Festival takes place the first weekend in June, and Fall Festival is held the first weekend in October. Festival hours are 9 A.M.–4 P.M. Festival admission is $5.00 for adults, $3.00 for children ages 13-18, and $2.00 for children ages 5-12.

Though the Turquoise Trail starts just outside Albuquerque in Tijeras, the bulk of it is in Santa Fe County, tracing the route of Highway 14, commonly known as North 14. The trail, designated a Scenic and Historic Area, connects the semi-ghost towns of Golden, Madrid, and Cerrillos (among others) along this leisurely behind-the-mountain path linking Albuquerque to Santa Fe.

The trail probably got its name from Mount Chalchihuitl, near Cerrillos, which contained a vast lode of the blue-green gemstones. The towns along the Turquoise Trail (sometimes known as the Ghost Town Trail) have a boom-and-bust mining legacy similar to that of towns in the southern part of the state. Mined in this area, in addition to turquoise, were coal, lead, copper, silver, and gold.

Though each of the spots along the Turquoise Trail has its own charms and history, the revived ghost town of **Madrid** (pronounced MAD-rid, unlike its namesake in Spain) is perhaps the most fun. Originally an old coal-mining town, Madrid all but died after the last mine shut down in the 1950s, when the demand for coal declined, thus leaving scores of similar, wooden "company houses" along this strip of North 14.

During the past fifteen or so years, Madrid has been rediscovered by artistic types and former hippies drawn to its funky charm. The successful revival of this onetime ghost town was even the subject of a "60 Minutes" spot in 1982. An old-fashioned general store (complete with a soda fountain) and a New Age crystal emporium join ranks with other small shops and restaurants. The commercial establishments share Madrid with the deserted and occupied houses that dot the main drag. Then too the weather is not the only thing that can get quite hot during the summer in Madrid—the outdoor Madrid jazz and blues concerts have become quite a popular weekend outing for folks from Albuquerque and Santa Fe.

Check out the **Mine Shaft Tavern** (505–473–0743) as a great example of a real mining-town bar. It's rustic, wooden, and dark and contains a large stone fireplace and a dart board. Hundreds of dollar bills sporting handwritten notes from visitors from all over the world are plastered on the wall above the bar. Live entertainment is also part of the Mine Shaft experience. In addition to drinks, the tavern serves up generous burgers and steaks, including buffalo steak when available, as well as sandwiches and several New Mexican dishes. The Tavern Burger is a good bet—a half-pound of ground beef laced and topped with blue cheese: delicious. The sign above the door says it all: WELCOME TO MADRID—MADRID HAS NO TOWN DRUNK, WE ALL TAKE TURNS.

Adjacent to the tavern you'll find the Old Coal Mine Museum, which contains the Engine House Theater. On weekends and holidays from Memorial Day through Labor Day, the theater presents hilarious melodrama productions. Booing, hissing, and throwing marshmallows (available at the door for a small fee) are encouraged. Shows change each season. Call (505) 473–0743 for current show times, admission charges, or reservations.

Taos County

Taos has long been a gathering place for creative people. Its reputation for seducing artists and nurturing their works began before the turn of the century and continues to this day. The legacy of the Taos Society of Artists and all those who followed lives on in Taos's many fine galleries—more per capita, in fact, than in any other city in the United States. The striking Taos Pueblo and acclaimed Taos Ski Valley have also brought this lovely little town worldwide attention.

Though there's more to Taos County than Taos itself, the city that grew around its now-famous plaza is a good place to start. As with Santa Fe, exploring Taos's downtown museums, galleries, and shops is best done on foot. Taos is actually composed of three communities, all with *Taos* in their names: There's Taos the town, Ranchos de Taos, and Taos Pueblo. First, Taos proper.

The Kit Carson Historic Museums consist of three different museums that collectively bring Taos's illustrious past to life—the Kit Carson Home, Martinez Hacienda, and Earnest L. Blumenschein Home. Admission to each museum is $3.00 for adults, $2.50 for seniors, and $6.00 for families (including up to three children; additional children, $2.00 each). Discounts apply if you want to visit more than one; you can purchase the multiple ticket at any of the museums.

True to the northern New Mexico tradition of "wonderful things lie hidden behind adobe walls," the **Kit Carson Home** lies behind a plain, storefrontlike facade. But history comes alive behind these adobe walls. Although Christopher "Kit" Carson was born in Kentucky in 1809, the legendary mountain man and scout made his home in Taos. He came to Taos in 1826 to become a trapper because the village was known as the center of the fur trade, owing to the abundance of beaver in the nearby mountain streams. In 1843, Carson bought this twelve-room adobe home as a wedding gift for his bride, Josefa Jaramillo. The home's rooms divide the museum into various exhibits. All periods of Taos's colorful history are depicted, in addition to a special display on Carson himself. Even Kit Carson's cradle is on display in the museum—and his grave is in nearby Kit Carson Park.

The Kit Carson Home is ½ block east of Taos Plaza on Kit Carson Road; (505) 758-0505. Summer hours are 8:00 A.M.–6:00 P.M. daily, and winter hours are 9:00 A.M.–5:00 P.M. daily.

For a view of Spanish colonial life in Taos, the **Martinez Hacienda** has no rivals. This fully restored compound sits defiantly on the banks of the Rio Pueblo just outside Taos as it did nearly 200 years ago. The sprawling, twenty-one-room home of Don Antonio Severino Martinez encloses two *placitas* (courtyard-type areas), has no exterior windows, and looks like a fort. In reality, it did serve as a fortress against the Apache and Comanche raids of the times.

Today the hacienda provides a glimpse back at the many components that made up the self-contained compound. A blacksmith shop, a tack room, a granary, and a weaving room have all been restored, as have living quarters with period furnishings. It's located 2 miles southeast of Taos Plaza on Highway 240; (505) 758–0505. It's open daily 9:00 A.M.–5:00 P.M.

The Blumenschein Home, the third component of the Kit Carson Historic Museums, is an art museum with the feel of a traditional museum in a homelike setting. The furnishings of the Blumenschein family of artists—Ernest; his wife, Mary; and their daughter, Helen—together with their paintings and those of other prominent Taos artists take visitors back to the glory days of art and culture in Taos.

Ernest Blumenschein was the cofounder of the now-legendary Taos Society of Artists. The story of how Blumenschein ended up in Taos—and thus put Taos on the art map—is well known. Blumenschein had originally heard about Taos from a fellow artist while studying in Paris in 1895. Later, during a trip from Denver to Mexico Blumenschein took with artist Bert Phillips, a wheel on their wagon broke north of Taos. After repairing the wheel in Taos, the artists became captivated by the valley, its inhabitants, and its brilliant light. They decided to stay and urged other artists to come to Taos as well. In 1912, Blumenschein, together with five other artists, founded the Taos Society of Artists, whose purpose was to enable its members as a group to exhibit their art in galleries throughout the country. In 1919, after spending many summers in Taos, Blumenschein and his young family moved from New York to Taos and purchased the home that was to become part of the Kit Carson Historic Museums.

The Blumenschein House is on Ledoux Street, 2 blocks west of Taos Plaza; (505) 758–0505. It's open daily 9:00 A.M.–5:00 P.M.

Farther west on Ledoux Street you'll find New Mexico's second-oldest museum, **The Harwood Foundation Museum,** which was founded in 1923 and has been operated by the University of New Mexico since 1935. The art museum contains paintings, drawings, prints, sculpture, and photographs by Taos artists from 1898 to the present. The Taos Society of Artists is well represented in this permanent collection. There's also an assortment of nineteenth century *retablos* (religious paintings on wood) that were given to the foundation by arts patron and writer Mabel Dodge Luhan. Special exhibitions of Taos artists and works from the University of New Mexico's collections are also displayed during the year.

The Harwood Foundation Museum is at 238 Ledoux Street; (505) 758–3063. Museum hours are Monday through Friday from 12:00 noon to 5:00 P.M. and Saturday from 10:00 A.M. to 4:00 P.M. There's no admission charge.

Like Santa Fe, Taos offers an abundance of distinctive lodging. The **Taos Inn** is the oldest hotel in town and the only one on the national and state registers of historic places. If you don't want to worry about getting around in your car, the Taos Inn is the best base from which to explore the downtown plaza area, including the shops, galleries, and cafes in the Bent Street District across the street. The inn, restored in 1982, has uniquely outfitted each of its forty guest rooms with pueblo-style furnishings, including hand-loomed Indian bedspreads; some also have adobe kiva fireplaces.

Doc Martin's, the inn's restaurant, is named after Taos's first doctor, who lived and practiced in part of what now accommodates the inn and restaurant. It specializes in innovative fish and pasta dishes and from 1985 through 1989 was honored by the *Wine Spectator* for having one of the most outstanding restaurant wine lists in the world. The inn's Adobe Bar is a comfortable, popular gathering place for the arts crowd; local musicians often provide entertainment as well. The bar's seating area flows into the lobby so that patrons can enjoy the atmosphere there as well.

Reservations are often hard to come by, so book early. Daily room rates range from $80 to $125. The Taos Inn is at 125 Paseo del Pueblo Norte; (505) 758–2233.

Not far from the plaza but sufficiently hidden is a wonderful inn with a fascinating past. The **Bed & Breakfast at the Mabel Dodge Luhan House** offers guest rooms in the original home as well as in a separate addition. But as the original estate of the Taos writer, designer, and champion of the southwestern creative arts movement, it's also worth exploring on its own. The existing 200-year-old structure was expanded to its present size of twenty-two rooms in 1922 by Antonio Luhan, Mabel's husband. Spanish colonial and Pueblo styles shine throughout.

Stories persist that the home is haunted by either the ghost of Mabel herself or that of a young Taos Pueblo girl. Apparitions aside, if these old adobe walls could talk, present-day visitors would gladly listen: Mabel entertained such guests as D. H. Lawrence, Willa Cather, Aldous Huxley, Georgia O'Keeffe, and Carl Jung here.

A whole different set of characters frequented the estate in the late 1960s and early 1970s, after actor Dennis Hopper purchased it when filming *Easy Rider* near Taos. Peter and Jane Fonda, Jack Nicholson, and Elizabeth Taylor were among Hopper's guests. (Some visitors would no doubt rather hear the walls talk about this period!)

The inn carries on in Mabel's tradition of hosting the creative crowd—many famous contemporary writers and artists enjoy the serenity and sense of history found here. Guests are served a breakfast buffet either in the spacious dining room or outside on the patio among the huge cottonwood, beech, and elm trees. Wine and cheese are often served in the afternoons.

Rates range from $55 to $125, with the two-bedroom gate

house going for $145. The bed-and-breakfast is located on Morada Street north of Kit Carson Road; (505) 758–9456.

Adjoining Taos on the south is the village of Ranchos de Taos, home of the **San Francisco de Asis Church,** built in 1850. No photographs are allowed of the mission church's interior, but you can click to your heart's desire outside. Photographers and painters have been capturing the image on film and canvas for more than a century, and oddly enough, it's the backside that most intrigues them. The unusual cruciform shape of the church, together with the soft contours of buttresses that support the adobe walls, is impressive enough, but the added element of the changing shadows combines to make the sight truly inspiring.

The mysterious *The Shadow of the Cross* painting, by Henri Ault, is on display in the rectory hall across from the church. The mystery of the portrait—which is of Christ on the shore of the Sea of Galilee—occurs when it is viewed in the dark: After about ten minutes the portrait becomes luminescent, outlining the figure while clouds over the left shoulder of Jesus form a shadow of a cross.

The painting was completed in 1896, years before the discovery of radium. Moreover, no luminous paint has so far been developed that will not darken and oxidize within a relatively short time. Ault claimed he didn't know why the painting changed in the dark. He even thought he was going crazy when he first went in his studio at night and discovered the luminosity.

The painting was first exhibited at the St. Louis World's Fair in 1904 and, after more than fifty years of exhibition in galleries throughout North America and Europe, is now at its permanent home. Every half-hour from 9:00 A.M. to 4:00 P.M. (Monday through Saturday) the church allows viewing of the spectacle by turning out the lights for visitors. There is no admission charge.

An adjacent gift shop sells religious articles, books, and cards Monday through Saturday, 9:00 A.M.–5:00 P.M. The plaza/parking area is lined with shops and galleries. The church is located just off Highway 68 in Ranchos de Taos; (505) 758–2754. It's open to visitors daily, except Sunday, 9:00 A.M.–4:00 P.M.

Just around the corner from San Francisco de Asis Church

you'll discover one of the more intimate bed-and-breakfasts, one doubling as the current home of noted Taos doll maker and sixth-generation Taoseña Patricia Martinez y Wayne de Peña. **Don Pascual Martinez Bed & Breakfast** has only two guest rooms, thereby concentrating for guests the personal attention provided by Patricia. A gracious hostess, Patricia has lived an incredibly interesting life and can help make the most of your visit to Taos. In 1988 she fulfilled her dream of running her own inn, after having served as a Harvey Girl at the El Tovar (Grand Canyon) and the Alvarado (Albuquerque) Harvey Houses (see Valencia County entry), in addition to holding various positions with the Hilton hotel chain in California.

Patricia's bed-and-breakfast is named after her grandfather, Pascual Martinez, one of the last generations of Martinez born in the Martinez Hacienda, now one of the Kit Carson Historic Museums. The inn's sitting area has a great selection of magazines and books on Indians, the Southwest, and southwestern architecture.

Don Pascual Martinez Bed & Breakfast is on Valerio Road, the road immediately south of San Francisco de Asis Church off Highway 68; (505) 758–7364. Rates are $55 and $65 per night.

Another secluded bed-and-breakfast can be found in the village of Talpa, just south of Ranchos de Taos. **Whistling Waters** is a bed-and-breakfast with a twist—it also includes a small gallery featuring the crafts of one of its owners, Jo Hutson. Jo and her husband, Al, originally bought the large, centuries-old adobe house to make into their home when they finally moved here from Kansas after twenty years of visiting northern New Mexico.

For travelers, it was worth the wait when the Hutsons opened their home as a bed-and-breakfast in 1988, after restoring it. (That seems to be the time when the bed-and-breakfast bug bit many New Mexican owners of historic homes.) All guest rooms open onto courtyards. The largest courtyard/garden area has a stream running through it, thus the inn's name.

The inn is enhanced by antiques collected by the Hutsons over the years, but the best part of the home is the small doorways typical of traditional old adobe homes. Most normal-size people just have to duck, but if you're extraordinarily large, this may not be the place for you. Doorways were constructed this way in the old days not because people were shorter but because the smaller openings conserved heat.

An address won't help you find Whistling Waters, so here are some directions (although protocol requires always calling first if you're interested in staying at a bed-and-breakfast): Take Highway 518 east off Highway 68 for 1½ miles and then take a left onto a paved road immediately past a school yard (not the Ranchos Elementary School you'll see earlier). When the road branches in three directions, take the sharpest left and after about a long block's distance you'll see the Whistling Waters sign on your right. Parking is across the street; (505) 758–7798. Daily room rates are $55, and the inn is closed during November.

Two miles north of Taos you'll find **Taos Pueblo,** New Mexico's most well known Indian pueblo. Besides its spectacular mountainside setting, Taos Pueblo gets this distinction because of its picturesque, multistory, apartmentlike architecture, which sets it apart from other pueblos. Taos Pueblo has been continuously inhabited for centuries, and the Taos Indians have lived at or near the present site for almost 1,000 years.

A walking tour is available to get a feel for the pueblo, its history, and its people. Aside from the obvious addition of tourists and the various Indian-owned shops catering to them, the pueblo looks much the way it did hundreds of years ago. The rapidly flowing, crystal-clear Rio Pueblo de Taos adds to the tranquillity of the setting and is still the only source of drinking water for Taos Pueblo residents.

While certain ceremonial dances and feast days are open to the public, here, as in most pueblos, some sacred activities are restricted to tribal members only. Therefore, if you don't want inadvertently to arrive at a closed pueblo during your visit, it's a good idea to call ahead.

Taos Pueblo is normally open to the public daily, 8:30 A.M.– 5:00 P.M. The following fees apply: admission, $5.00 per car or $2.00 per person; still cameras, $5.00; sketching, $15.00; painting, $35.00; movie or video cameras, $10.00. Taos Pueblo is 2 miles north of Taos off Highway 68; (505) 758–4604.

Taos Indian Horse Ranch, an Indian-owned venture near the pueblo, is popular with horse-loving visitors. The ranch, with 80,000 acres of riding trails, provides various rides and excursions. In the winter, traditional sleigh rides are given over breathtaking terrain and come complete with Indian storytellers, music, camp fires, and marshmallow roasts.

Most of the trail guides are Taos Pueblo Indians who are master riders. The ranch features horses selected for their ability to ride responsively to the novice rider. The place has been owned and operated by Cesario Stormstar Gomez and his family for twenty years.

Tour prices range from $25.00 to $165.00. Sleigh rides cost from $27.50 per person for the family rate to $175.50 for the exclusive honeymooner ride. Because all tours are by appointment only, call (505–758–3212) for reservations, as well as to get directions.

Taos County's other pueblo, **Picuris Pueblo,** is not so well known to tourists and is thus more representative of most New Mexico pueblos. Some feel it offers visitors a more authentic New Mexico Indian experience than the very visible Taos Pueblo.

Because Picuris Pueblo is located in a hidden valley, it was the last of New Mexico's pueblos to be discovered by Spanish explorers. Despite its relative isolation, Picuris is quite receptive to visitors. The Picuris Pueblo Museum displays pottery, beadwork, and weavings. The Hidden Valley Shop and Restaurant are also on the pueblo. Every August 10 the pueblo celebrates St. Lorenzo Feast Day, which is open to the public.

There is no fee to visit the pueblo or the museum. There are, however, fees for self-guided and guided tours ($1.75 and $2.75 per person, respectively), as well as for fishing or camping permits. The pueblo is open to visitors Monday through Friday from 8:00 A.M. to 7:00 P.M. and weekends from 9:00 A.M. to 7:00 P.M. To get to Picuris Pueblo, take Highway 75 east for 13 miles off of Highway 68; (505) 587-2957.

For more than sixteen years Jim and Leslie Leahy have been catering to eager shoppers at their **Overland Sheepskin Company** north of Taos. The huge, barnlike showroom is packed with an extensive line of sheepskin and leather products—coats, rugs, vests, slippers, mittens, and more. The grounds are almost as attractive as the showroom: In the summer and early fall, flower gardens add to the attractive meadow scene, with Taos Mountain as the backdrop; grazing sheep complete the picture.

The factory, which looks more like an inn, is also located on the grounds, as is a second shop featuring pelts. The Leahys now have three other locations (Santa Fe, San Francisco, and Napa Valley), but it all started in Taos. Overland Sheepskin Company is located about 3 miles north of Taos Plaza on Highway 522; (505) 758–8822. It's open daily 8:00 A.M.–8:00 P.M.

The **Millicent Rogers Museum** is one of the finest and most specialized museums in the area. The private, non-profit institution celebrates the art and culture of the Native American and Hispanic peoples of the Southwest. Built around the extensive collection of the late Millicent Rogers, the museum is a living memorial to this woman who took it upon herself to collect and preserve what she recognized as the rapidly vanishing arts of the area's people during the late 1940s and early 1950s.

In addition to a representative collection of Native American and Hispanic arts, the museum boasts the most important public holding of the lifework of San Ildefonso Pueblo's most famous potter, Maria Martinez, and her talented family (see Santa Fe County entry).

The museum is 4 miles north of Taos, just off Highway 522 (turn left before the blinking light and follow the signs); (505) 758–2462. The museum is open daily 9:00 A.M.–5:00 P.M. Admission is $3.00 for adults, $1.00 for children ages six to sixteen, and $2.00 for seniors.

After absorbing some of the area's culture at the Millicent Rogers Museum, head over to the **Rio Grande Gorge Bridge** for a spectacular though slightly unnerving experience. There's a parking area on each side of the bridge. From either one you can walk across the bridge—a narrow sidewalk runs alongside the highway—which spans the 1,200-foot-wide gorge. Midway across, a small lookout platform on each side allows you to peer down 600 feet into the gorge to the wild Rio Grande. Yes, there is a railing.

The bridge is on U.S. Highway 64, about 11 miles west of the 64/522 junction just north of Taos. No hours, no phone, no admission fee, no rest rooms.

Fort Burgwin, an 1850s fort south of Taos that protected past residents from Apache and Comanche raids, was rescued from ruin and restored by Southern Methodist University and opened as an external campus of the school in 1974. Though the Fort Burgwin Research Center may be just school to students fortunate enough to study here, to the rest of us Fort Burgwin really comes to life during summer. Each July and August Fort Burgwin hosts a summer festival of music, theater, and art. But the best news is that it's all free. Call (505) 758–8322 for performance dates and times.

The **Red River State Trout Hatchery,** near the community of Questa, is one of those rare functional places that double as tourist attractions. New Mexico is fortunate to have many hatcheries, thus ensuring a steady supply of fish to stock the state's many streams, rivers, and lakes.

Located within the Carson National Forest, the hatchery offers a delightful setting. It was originally built in 1941 and then totally reconstructed during 1985–86. Pick up a brochure in the unstaffed visitor center to follow the self-guided tour of the hatchery facilities. You'll see huge rainbow trout at the display ponds, as well as view the fish in various stages of growth, from their beginning as eggs to their development into fully mature trout. The hatchery, New Mexico's largest, produces 300,000 pounds of trout annually.

Picnic tables dot the scenic 2-mile drive on Highway 515, which connects the hatchery to Highway 522, 2½ miles south of Questa; (505) 586–0222. Visitors are welcome 8:00 A.M.– 5:00 P.M. daily. There's no admission charge.

After you've heard the fish story—uh, the story of fish—at the hatchery, continue on to Questa and fill up on the fine fare at El Seville Restaurant, a local landmark for sixteen years. Though the menu is varied and extensive, the authentic New Mexican combo plates are the best bet. El Seville offers freshly prepared tortilla chips—the best I've had—with its New Mexican entrees. Two combo dinners, including the chips and homemade sopaipillas, can be had for about $15. Get a window table for stunning mountain views. El Seville is not fancy, but owner Virgil Martinez, Sr., knows how to consistently satisfy his loyal customers.

El Seville is at the junction of Highway 522 and Highway 38 in Questa; (505) 586–0300. It's open 6:00 A.M.–8:00 P.M. daily.

Taos County also offers an array of choices for the outdoor

adventurer. From world-class skiing at **Taos Ski Valley** to white-water river rafting in the Rio Grande Gorge and everything in between, Taos's incredible scenery provides an inspiring setting during every season.

Taos Ski Valley is simply New Mexico's finest ski resort. Built in the European tradition and nurtured by the late Ernie Blake, the father of New Mexico skiing, Taos Ski Valley delivers an extraordinary ski experience. *Skiing* magazine says, "The secret of Taos is in the mixture. Take European style, southwestern flavor, perfect snow and exquisite mountains and stir. . . . Taos Ski Valley is a resort to fall in love with, whatever your ability." And the *London Times* says, "Without any argument the best ski resort in the world. Small, intimate and endlessly challenging, Taos simply has no equal." Enough said.

Ideally, ski season runs from Thanksgiving through early April. Lift prices range from $12 for a children's half-day ticket to $32 for an adult's full-day ticket. Taos Ski Valley is just minutes away from Taos on Highway 150 via Highway 522; (505) 776–2291.

Though the protected stretch of wild and scenic Rio Grande extends 48 miles, the visitor center and **Wild Rivers Recreation Area** of this region are located north of Questa. This segment of the Rio Grande was officially protected when Congress passed the Wild and Scenic Rivers Act in 1968. It's quite-deserted country, but when the weather is fair, canoeists and kayakers flock here.

The 18,000-acre recreation area, close to the center of the stretch, contains six maintained hiking trails and eight campsites on the rim and in the canyon. Guided hikes and regular camp-fire presentations are offered during the summer. There are picnic facilities if you just want to peer into the vast starkness of the gorge—and you might just see a soaring bald eagle.

To get to the visitor center, head 3 miles north of Questa on Highway 522 and then go west on Highway 538 for 8 miles. You'll see signs; (505) 758–8851. Visitor center hours are 9:00 A.M.–5:00 p.m, Memorial Day weekend through Labor Day weekend; however, the Wild Rivers Recreation Area is open year-round for camping, hiking, fishing, and sightseeing. Various fees apply.

For the less active outdoor enthusiast—or for active ones just wanting a break and some breathtaking scenery—there's The Enchanted Circle drive. The Enchanted Circle is the name for the communities and countryside surrounding Wheeler Peak, New Mexico's highest spot, at 13,161 feet. The loop, which involves several highways, connects the towns of Taos, Arroyo Hondo, Questa, and Red River in Taos County with Angel Fire and Eagle Nest in Colfax County (see Colfax County entry). Although the views of many areas in The Enchanted Circle are spectacular all year, they really shine during autumn—most specifically during late September and early October, when the aspens give their all before colder weather forces them to drop their amber leaves.

The most scenic stretch involves taking U.S. Highway 64 in Taos northeast to Eagle Nest and then Highway 38 north to Red River. At a leisurely pace, the drive should take less than two hours.

Red River is an unabashedly successful tourist town charmed with a beautiful storybook setting. Like so many western resort areas (Aspen and Telluride come to mind), Red River started out as a mining town in the 1800s but was savvy enough to capitalize on its mountains and snow when the mines played out. Winter visitors enjoy the family-oriented Red River Ski Area, and year-round visitors enjoy the shopping, food, and scenery. Red River has its own funky appeal, blending a European-chalet style with a big dose of the Old West. Red River is on Highway 38, between Questa and Eagle Nest.

The tiny southeastern Taos County town of Ojo Caliente possesses a marvelous secret bubbling up from the earth. And **Ojo Caliente Mineral Springs,** one of North America's oldest health resorts, is here to take advantage of it. This is not your plush Scottsdale- or Palms Springs-type resort. Far from it. But then again, neither are the prices. The facilities and accommodations at Ojo Caliente ("Hot Spring") are rather plain and limited, but this is the place in northern New Mexico to visit if you want to relax—totally.

Separate women's and men's bathhouses are equipped with pools and tubs for soaking in the natural therapeutic mineral waters that have been attracting folks to this area for probably 2,000 years, starting with the ancestors to New Mexico's

Pueblo Indians. The Spanish explorer Cabeza de Vaca described his journey to Ojo Caliente this way:

> *The greatest treasure that I found these strange people to possess are some hot springs which burst out at the foot of a mountain that gives evidence of being an active volcano. So powerful are the chemicals contained in this water that the inhabitants have a belief that they were given to them by their gods. These springs I have named Ojo Caliente.*

Lithia spring pump at Ojo Caliente

Hotel and cabin accommodations are available, and the on-site Mineral Springs Restaurant specializes in healthful meals featuring fish, chicken, and vegetarian fare as well as New Mexican foods. But the mineral waters are the focus at the resort: iron and arsenic for soaking; iron, arsenic, lithia, and soda for drinking. (*Note:* The arsenic mineral water has only a trace of arsenic and is said to benefit those with arthritis, rheumatism, and stomach ulcers as well as to promote relief of burns and eczema.) Various massages, herbal wraps, facials, and rubs are also available.

The resort is ¼ mile west of the town of Ojo Caliente on Highway 285; (505) 583–2233. Winter hours (starting the day after Thanksgiving) are from 10:00 A.M. to 7:00 P.M. Monday through Friday and from 8:00 A.M. to 7:00 P.M. Saturday and Sunday. Summer hours (starting the day after Easter) are from 8:00 A.M. to 7:00 P.M. daily. Bed-bath-and-breakfast accommodations range from $34.00 to $53.00; soaks, including wraps, are $6.50 weekdays and $8.50 weekends and holidays.

Off the Beaten Path in Central New Mexico

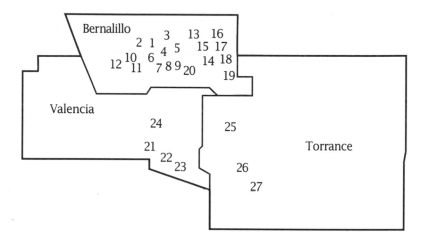

1. Old Town
2. Casas de Sueños
3. Indian Pueblo Cultural Center
4. KiMo Theatre
5. La Posada de Albuquerque
6. M. & J. Restaurant & Sanitary Tortilla Factory
7. Tamarind Institute
8. Nob Hill District
9. Classic Century Square
10. Anderson Valley Vineyards
11. Rio Grande Nature Center
12. Petroglyph Park
13. La Luz Trail
14. Sandia Peak Tramway

15. Sandia Crest
16. Tinkertown Museum
17. Pine Cone Bed and Breakfast
18. Elaine's
19. Sierra Farms
20. National Atomic Museum
21. Valencia County Historical Museum
22. P & M Chavez Farm Museum
23. Valencia Flour Mill
24. Luna Mansion
25. Tajique-Torreon Loop
26. Salinas National Monument
27. Rancho Bonito

Central New Mexico

Compared with the other six regions in the state, central New Mexico is small in area but big on influence. Boasting the state's only true urban area (but also very rural sectors), central New Mexico combines facets of all the other regions in the state because it borders them all. That there's much to experience in this region is partly why the largest chunk of the state's population calls central New Mexico home.

Bernalillo County

Because the Albuquerque metropolitan area contains approximately one-third of New Mexico's residents, it tends to dominate Bernalillo County. And, as the state's largest city, Albuquerque has its share of attractions to please a variety of interests.

Albuquerque was founded in 1706 by Don Francisco Cuervo y Valdes in honor of the Duke of Alburquerque, Viceroy of New Spain. The first "r" was later dropped, but Albuquerque is still known as The Duke City. The place Valdes actually designated "San Francisco de Alburquerque" is **Old Town,** just west of downtown.

In addition to its status as a historic zone of Albuquerque, Old Town is home for many families whose ancestors settled the area. On the surface, the shops around Old Town's plaza seem to cater only to tourists, but the fun part of exploring Old Town is venturing off the plaza into the side streets. There you'll find an array of fun-to-explore shops, galleries, and restaurants. Old Town's plaza is the site of the annual Christmas Eve Luminaria Tour. Here, tens of thousands of luminarias (single candles set in a bed of sand at the bottom of small paper bags) create a golden glow on this special night at the place where Albuquerque began.

Parking is free around the plaza, if you can find a spot, but off the plaza are several parking lots that offer parking for $1.00–$2.00. Old Town is located near the intersection of Central Avenue and Rio Grande Boulevard. Most retail establishments are open seven days a week and maintain normal business hours, while others stay open later. As with many destinations in New Mexico, Old Town is most crowded during "tourist season," which basically means summer. If your schedule is flexible, fall and winter (after Christmas) are the most pleasant times to visit.

If you're interested in buying Native American Indian jewelry and crafts, there are, in addition to the shops around Old Town's plaza, two stores nearby that offer discount pricing on jewelry, pottery, kachina dolls, drums, and other authentic crafts. Gus's Trading Company is across the street from Old Town's plaza at 2026 Central SW (505–843–6381), and Palms Trading Company is also close at 1504 Lomas NW (505–247–8507). Gus's is open Monday through Saturday from 9:00 A.M. to 5:30 P.M. and Sunday from 10:00 A.M. to 5:00 P.M.; Palms Trading Company is open Monday through Saturday from 9:00 A.M. to 5:30 P.M.

A new bed-and-breakfast inn, called **Casas de Sueños** ("Houses of Dreams"), opened near Old Town in 1990. The inn, which has several garden areas and courtyards, is within walking distance to many Old Town and downtown attractions, such as the New Mexico Museum of Natural History, The Albuquerque Museum, and the Rio Grande Zoo. The futuristic entry building designed by noted Albuquerque architect Bart Prince contrasts with the traditional old adobe structures that compose the inn. Accommodations range from one- and· two-bedroom suites to private casitas, many with kitchens and fireplaces.

Casas de Sueños is at 310 Rio Grande SW; (505) 247–4560. Rates range from $65 to $200.

The **Indian Pueblo Cultural Center** near Old Town is *the* place to go to experience the art, history, and culture of New Mexico's nineteen pueblos (and one, Hopi Pueblo, in Arizona)—before venturing out to explore any of them. The center is owned and operated by the Pueblo Tribes of New Mexico and houses a fine museum and a restaurant that features New Mexican and Pueblo Indian dishes. The museum is divided into three main sections: the prehistoric, the historic, and the contemporary.

The center also contains gift shops—some of which are more like galleries—offering authentic Indian pottery, sculp-

87

ture, paintings, rugs, sand paintings, kachina dolls, and jewelry. Traditional Indian dance performances, alternated among the pueblos, are held on weekends in summer at 11:00 A.M. and 2:00 P.M.

The Indian Pueblo Cultural Center is at 2401 Twelfth Street NW, just north of I-40; (505) 843-7270. Admission to the museum is $2.50 for adults, $1.50 for seniors, and $1.00 for students. Museum and gift shops are open daily from 9:00 A.M. to 5:30 P.M., and the restaurant is open daily from 7:30 A.M. to 3:30 P.M.

Like many cities' downtown areas in the past two decades, Albuquerque's downtown area is experiencing a renaissance of sorts as citizens once again take pride in their city's center. A spot worth a look during your tour of downtown is the **KiMo Theatre,** built in 1927 in the pueblo-deco style and later restored by the city. The theater hosts a wide range of performances and is the Albuquerque stage for New Mexico Repertory Theatre productions. The KiMo Theatre is at 423 Central NW; (505) 848-1374.

Listed on the National Register of Historic Places, **La Posada de Albuquerque** was built in 1939 by Conrad Hilton, his first hotel in his home state. Among the hotel's claims to fame is its designation as the first air-conditioned building in Albuquerque and as the honeymoon hotel for Mr. Hilton and his bride Zsa Zsa Gabor. La Posada, remodeled to its former glory in 1984, includes a spacious lobby bar and a classic coffee shop—both favorites of local downtowners. La Posada also has a first-class restaurant, Eulalia's, which features a wait staff singing Broadway musicals. La Posada is at 125 Second Street NW; (505) 242-9090 or (800) 777-1901. Room rates range from $68 to $225.

A great place to break for lunch downtown is **M. & J. Restaurant & Sanitary Tortilla Factory.** Located on the fringe of the downtown core, M. & J.'s offers traditional New Mexican fare at reasonable prices. Its red chile and green chile are among the city's most flavorful and hottest— the reason the restaurant provides a pitcher of ice water at each table.

Posted on the walls above the booths are letters, cards, and even messages scrawled on napkins from satisfied diners from all over the globe. They all sing the praises of this fiery food and the friendly people. You don't stay in the business for thirty years in the supercompetitive Albuquerque restaurant market unless you keep 'em coming back, something M. & J.'s owners, Bea and Jake Montoya, have always known. The wait staff keeps the complimentary homemade chips and salsa coming before and during the meal, and despite the filling nature of the cuisine, everything's heart-healthy here: The restaurant uses only cholesterol-free oil.

M. & J.'s is at 403 Second Street SW; (505) 242–4890. It's open Monday through Saturday, 9:00 A.M.–4:00 P.M.; evening hours are planned.

College campuses and the areas surrounding them are usually some of the most interesting places in a city, and the University of New Mexico in Albuquerque is no different. As the largest university in the state, UNM is located along Central Avenue (old Route 66) east of downtown. A stroll around UNM's campus reveals perhaps the finest examples of pueblo revival-style architecture. These buildings were designed by New Mexico's most famous architect, the late John Gaw Meem of Santa Fe, who served as consulting architect for UNM from 1933 to 1959. Zimmermann Library, Scholes Hall, and Alumni Chapel are three of the Meem firm's most striking designs on campus and are worth a look and a few photographs. The beautifully landscaped duck-pond area in the campus's center, adjacent to Zimmermann Library, is an idyllic spot for a country picnic in the middle of the city.

Tamarind Institute, housed in a nondescript building across Central Avenue from the university, is much more than a division of UNM. It's a unique educational facility dedicated to the fine art of collaborative lithography. And it gives the best tour in Albuquerque. The good news is that the tour is free. The bad news is that it only happens once a month—the first Friday of each month at 1:00 P.M.

If you didn't know a thing about collaborative lithography before your visit to Tamarind, you'll be an expert after the two-hour tour, which includes viewing an Emmy-nominated documentary produced by the institute, a briefing by the director, and a staff-guided tour of the facility.

Tamarind began in 1960 in Los Angeles as the Tamarind Lithography Workshop. Its purpose was to rescue collaborative lithography from becoming a lost art in the United States by training a pool of master printers to work with artists. After ten years in Los Angeles, Tarmarind, supported by substantial Ford Foundation grants, moved to Albuquerque in 1970 to become self-sustaining and continue the goals established in California.

If your visit doesn't coincide with a tour, you can still view some of the finished works—a small gallery at the institute displays selected lithographs. Some are available for purchase, and once you understand the lengthy collaborative lithography process, you'll understand the prices.

Tamarind Institute is at 108 Cornell Avenue SE; (505) 277–3901. Gallery hours are 9:00 A.M.–5:00 P.M. Monday through Friday.

The **Nob Hill District,** just east of UNM along Central Avenue near Carlisle Boulevard, re-creates that old Route 66 ambience. This recently revived section of Albuquerque showcases antiques shops, vintage-clothing stores, other shops, theaters, and cafes, all interspersed among more practical businesses to create an eclectic mix perfect for a Saturday-afternoon stroll. Among the places not to miss are Scalo, a northern Italian grill; Bow Wow Records; the In Crowd, a shop with trendy clothing and a fantastic postcard selection; and PeaceCraft, a nonprofit shop featuring handmade goods from Third World nations.

Although individual antiques stores abound in and around the Nob Hill District (mostly along Central and Morningside avenues), the largest selection of antique and collector items under one roof is at **Classic Century Square.** This old department-store building houses three levels of antiques, collectibles, furniture, glassware, books, jewelry, and other items in more than 125 wall-less shops. There's an exceptionally large collection of vintage dolls in one section of the complex. You could spend a whole afternoon browsing and still not see everything.

Classic Century Square is at 4616 Central Avenue SE, just east of San Mateo Boulevard; (505) 265–3161. It's open Monday through Saturday from 10:00 A.M. to 6:00 P.M. and Sunday from 12:00 noon to 5:00 P.M.

Albuquerque's rural North Valley, situated near the Rio Grande, contains some of the area's most fertile land, planted with apple orchards, alfalfa fields, extensive gardens—and grapes for wine at **Anderson Valley Vineyards.** The award-winning winery, near the vineyards, offers wine tastings, in addition to a gift shop selling wine- and gourmet-related items. An outdoor patio overlooking alfalfa fields is a great spot at which to enjoy a picnic with friends—accompanied by a bottle of Anderson Valley wine, of course.

Anderson Valley was started in 1984 by the late Maxie Anderson and his wife. Maxie was a famous hot-air-balloon pilot who set world records with a transcontinental balloon flight (along with his son Kris) and a transatlantic flight (with Ben Abruzzo). His family continues the wine-making tradition he began.

The wine tastings and tours of the winery cost $1.00, which is applied toward the purchase of a bottle of wine. Tours are held whenever people come by in the winter and hourly in the summer. Anderson Valley's tasting room is at 4920 Rio Grande Boulevard NW; (505) 344-7266. It's open Tuesday through Sunday, 12:00 noon–5:00 P.M.

Hot-air ballooning is extremely popular in New Mexico because of the state's predictable weather and clear skies. To celebrate this colorful sport, New Mexico's largest city hosts the Albuquerque International Balloon Fiesta each October.

Balloonists and spectators come from all over the world to take part in the nine-day event, which draws more than 100,000 spectators. The mass ascensions on the four weekend mornings during the fiesta are worth an early rising (while it's still dark out) for the trek to Balloon Fiesta Park, located on Alameda Boulevard off I–25. Up to 600 balloons take off to thousands of "oohs and ahs," while amateur and professional photographers click away at what has surpassed Pasadena's Tournament of Roses Parade as the most photographed annual event in the world.

In addition to the mass ascensions, the yearly Balloon Glow has become quite a popular event. After sunset, hundreds of inflated hot-air balloons fire up in synchronized patterns to create huge spheres of colorful, glowing light. If you make it to Albuquerque for the fiesta, don't miss the Balloon Glow. Another fun ballooning event during the fiesta is the Special Shapes Rodeo, limited to those balloons tailored a bit differently from the usual inverted-teardrop configuration. You'll see Mickey Mouse, the Planter's Peanut Man, a Pepsi can, a cow jumping over a moon, and scores more of the huge floating representations of familiar items.

The fiesta begins the first weekend each October. For more information, call (505) 821–1000.

New Mexico is a nature lover's paradise, and Albuquerque fits right in. The **Rio Grande Nature Center** in Albuquerque's North Valley lies, as its name implies, along the Rio Grande, and is a wonderful place for leisurely walks or brisk hikes. The outside part of the center consists of 270 acres of riverside forest and meadows that include stands of hundred-year-old cottonwoods, among other trees, and a 3-acre pond. The *bosque,* as wooded areas are called in the Southwest, is threaded with 2 miles of trails whose unobtrusive signs identify the various forms of plant life.

The inside part of the center contains self-guided exhibits that provide insight into the natural, historical, and social implications of the Rio Grande. In the library area, there's also a glassed-in viewing room from which you can observe the wildlife at the pond without being noticed. A sign hanging here, THIS WEEK'S VISITORS, lists the species of birds and other animals that have been spotted recently.

Nature walks and children's hikes are scheduled, and you can borrow a pair of binoculars if you have a photo ID. Although the center makes for an enjoyable outing throughout the year, weekdays during fall and winter are especially tranquil. It's not—as a sign at the center's entrance prominently points out—a place to have a picnic, ride your bike or horse, run or jog, or walk your dog.

The Rio Grande Nature Center is at 2901 Candelaria NW (where Candelaria dead-ends); (505) 344–7240. It's open daily 10:00 A.M.–5:00 P.M. (And they mean it: Cars left in the parking lot after 5:00 P.M. will be locked in.) Admission is 25 cents, with children under six admitted at no charge.

The west side of Albuquerque is often referred to as the West Mesa because, well, it *is* a mesa. It rises out of Albuquerque's valley to form a wonderfully flat horizon (except for a few dormant volcanoes, for visual interest) perfect for the setting sun to sink into. It's on the West Mesa that you'll find **Petroglyph Park.** (Congress has appropriated money to turn this into Petroglyph National Monument, but that's a couple of years down the road.) At a distance, Petroglyph

Park is a barren, unimpressive pile of rocks on a hill. But look a little closer and you'll see why the place got its name: The rocks are "decorated" with ancient Indian petroglyphs, or prehistoric rock art. Markers along the trails indicate and interpret the drawings. The monument is a fun place to spend a couple of hours on a sunny, brisk winter day. It may be too hot, though, because of the lack of shade, for some folks during the peak of summer.

To get to the petroglyphs, take I–40 west and exit onto North Coors Road. Proceed $\frac{7}{10}$ mile to Sequoia Road. Turn left and go 3 miles to the park; (505) 897–8814. It's open daily 8:00 A.M.–5:00 P.M. Admission is $1.00 per vehicle.

Although most of the unique places lie near the older parts of town—Old Town, downtown, the university area, the North Valley—there's much to see in the "newer" parts of Albuquerque. The Heights, specifically the Far Northeast Heights, are blessed with the Sandia Mountains, which form a lovely backdrop for the city while bordering its east side. The Spaniards named the mountains *Sandia,* which means "watermelon," because of the red color they turn when hit by the setting sun.

To explore the Sandias from Albuquerque, consider a hike on **La Luz Trail.** In Spanish, the name of this scenic 8-mile trail means "The Light." The trail, known as the site of the La Luz Trail Run held each August, begins at the Juan Tabo recreation area and follows the western slope of the Sandias. The well-marked trail averages a 12 percent grade over the 3,700-foot-rise; thus, the three- to five-hour hike is quite a workout.

Bring along plenty of water, snacks, and matches, as well as a flashlight and bad-weather gear. It gets quite brisk at the higher elevations, even during the summer months, so dress appropriately. Because of temperature extremes, winter is not the best time to tackle La Luz. Being prepared and using common sense cannot be stressed enough, as evidenced by the media attention given to the several hikers per year who fall or become stranded. For this reason, be sure to tell someone where you are going when you hike La Luz.

From I–25 in north Albuquerque, exit at Tramway Boulevard and go 4 miles east to the Juan Tabo turnoff. Follow the road to the trailhead.

The foothills of the Sandias provide a wonderful vantage point from which to view the spectacular sunsets for which New Mexico is famous. And a comfortable spot for the nightly show is the Firehouse Restaurant at the Tram. The Firehouse is nestled in the foothills at the base of the **Sandia Peak Tramway,** the world's longest aerial tramway, which will whisk you to the top of 10,400-foot Sandia Peak in about fifteen minutes. At the top of the tram you'll find another restaurant, High Finance, which has an eagle's-eye view of Albuquerque. In addition to serving fine food, High Finance is also a great place for skiers to take a break at the top of the lifts on the other side of the mountain at Sandia Peak Ski Area.

Tram rides are popular at all times of the year, but be aware that winter temperatures can be more than thirty degrees colder at the top, which doesn't make for very comfortable sight-seeing. Still, you can always hang out at High Finance and have a cup of coffee or a glass of wine. And if you're lucky, you might see a brave hang-glider pilot take the plunge—harnessed in his glider, we hope—toward the Rio Grande valley 1 mile below.

The Tramway (505–298–8518) is at 38 Tramway Road off Tramway Boulevard. Though there's no set schedule, the tram runs about every twenty to thirty minutes from 9:00 A.M. to 9:00 P.M. daily (noon to 9:00 P.M. on Wednesdays). Round-trip tickets are $10.00 for adults and $7.50 for children and seniors. Each tram departure is announced in the Firehouse Restaurant, so you can wait for your "flight" in the bar if you like. Both restaurants give discounts on tram rides when you dine with them.

The top and the other side of the Sandias are also worth exploring. It's amazing that although most Albuquerque residents see the Sandias every day, many of them still don't realize that they can *drive* to the very top—**Sandia Crest,** at 10,678 feet—in less than an hour via I–40 and the Sandia Crest Highway (Highway 536), which has been designated a National Scenic Byway; it's also the highest scenic drive in the Southwest. At the top, you'll find things a lot different than they were back "on the ground." Here, it's a lot cooler, which is refreshing during the summer; even so, you might want to bring a sweater or light jacket.

The views from the crest are incredible. It's hard to imagine that the "small town" over the edge is bustling Albuquerque. The city becomes a distant, twinkling fairyland after sunset. From the observation deck at the summit you can see more than 15,000 square miles of central New Mexico. You're not totally isolated, however: The Sandia Crest House—a combination gift shop, restaurant, and all-around base for hiking and cross-country skiing in the winter—is perched at the top.

Once you've conquered the crest, check out **Tinkertown Museum** on your way back down the mountain. The museum is subtitled "Wood-Carved Miniature Village & Glass Bottle House" and is a place not to be missed. Even for people who don't think they like this sort of thing, I repeat, it's a place not to be missed!

Billed as "a collection of collections," Tinkertown explores a world gone by as well as a slightly skewed one that never existed. You'll get a month's worth of smiles after an hour of following the arrows directing you through the displays of miniature exhibits, including a general store and three-ring circus. Some displays involve mechanical action that brings the figures to life. You'll also see ghost-town relics from New Mexico's Billy the Kid Country, as well as "The Wishing Buddha," accompanied by a sign that reads WISH FOR PEACE ON EARTH, NOT JUST A PIECE OF THE ACTION. The self-guided tour takes you through a structure built out of glass bottles as the sounds of old-time frontier music further remove you from time and place.

Tinkertown is the result of more than thirty years of tinkering by owner-creator-curator-artist Ross Ward. And just when you're wondering when he found the time to do all this, you'll see his motto posted on the wall: I DID ALL THIS WHILE YOU WERE WATCHING TV!

Tinkertown is 1²⁄10 miles up Highway 536 off Highway 14; (505) 281–5233. It's open daily, 9:00 A.M.–6:00 P.M., from April to November. Admission is $2.00 for adults and 50 cents for children ages four to eighteen, while children under four get a free peek at Ward's world.

Near Tinkertown, you'll find the **Pine Cone Bed and Breakfast.** Located on the ground floor of innkeeper Valerie Foreman's home, the Pine Cone offers an Albuquerque-area alternative to the sometimes-sterile hotel rooms on the other side of the mountain. Although Valerie has owned the inn for only two of its seven years of operation, she adds personal touches to make her guests feel special. A chilled bottle of New Mexico wine, lighted candles, and a fire in the fireplace often greet guests of the Pine Cone.

If weather permits, Valerie will serve breakfast outdoors on her patio, which backs up to the Cibola National Forest. Guests can use the inn as a ski lodge during the winter or, if it's not too cold, can just lounge in the hammock near the fountain out back, enjoying the sounds and smells of the forest.

The Pine Cone is at 13 Tejano Canyon Road, 1 mile up Highway 536 (on the left) off Highway 14; (505) 281-1384. Room/suite rates range from $65 to $130.

Another bed-and-breakfast inn on this side of the mountain perched in the Sandias is **Elaine's.** Elaine Nelson O'Neil built this lodge-pole pine home for herself about ten years ago and turned the top two floors of it into a bed-and-breakfast in 1988. The common area of the no-smoking-permitted inn has a vaulted ceiling, a huge stone fireplace, and an upright piano, all with a fantastic alpine view through floor-to-ceiling windows.

Rates run from $60 to $82 per night. To get to Elaine's, take the Tijeras/Cedar Crest (Highway 14) exit off I-40 and, as you drive under I-40, check your odometer; then go 4.1 miles north on Highway 14. Turn left at the Turquoise Trail Campground (approximately 1 mile past Bella Vista Restaurant). Go straight on the dirt road approximately ½ mile. Turn left at the T. As you enter the gate marked "Snowline Estates," you'll see Elaine's on your right at the top of the hill. Follow the road up the hill and around the corner; (505) 281-2467.

Before going back to Albuquerque, head out east on Highway 337 near the eastern border of Bernalillo County to **Sierra Farms.** The farm is home to the goats that produce the milk Valentin and Carmen Sanchez make into a delectable array of cheese products—traditional and specialty cheeses, cheesecake, and even a tasty chocolate-piñon-ricotta confection.

Val and Carmen moved to the tranquil Manzano Mountains

(the range adjacent to the Sandias) from Albuquerque in 1976 to build a herd of dairy goats in hope of one day opening their own dairy. In 1986, Sierra Farms's Queso de Sanchez ("Sanchez's Cheese") was presented to the public in the cheese-tasting room—and the public ate it up.

In addition to sampling and sales, Sierra Farms offers self-guided and group tours on which you'll get to see those adorable kids. It's also a great place to take kids of the human variety, for there are picnic facilities and even a children's garden area during the summer. And if you want to see the goats milked, by machine, plan to come out at 6:00 A.M or P.M. Most folks choose the latter.

Individual tours are free, but there's a nominal fee for group tours depending on the size—call ahead for reservations for these. Sierra Farms is open to the public 8:00 A.M.–8:00 P.M., Tuesday through Sunday; during the summer, it's also open on Monday holidays. Sierra Farms is just off Highway 337, 17.2 miles south from the Tijeras/Cedar Crest exit off I–40. You'll see the sign; (505) 281–5061.

Back in Albuquerque, the **National Atomic Museum** stands apart from the city's more traditional museums. It is a serious but fun place to learn about the history and development of nuclear power. Though the thought of nuclear anything makes many people cringe, even devout pacifists can enjoy this fascinating display, which objectively portrays New Mexico's nuclear heritage: the development of the first atom bomb during the 1940s in Los Alamos (see Los Alamos County entry) and, subsequently, the first atomic blast at the Trinity Site (see Socorro County entry). The museum takes you through these historical developments and displays nuclear (but nonradioactive!) artifacts. A full range of military applications, including rockets and a B-52 bomber, is the focus of a large inside/outside exhibit.

The museum is on Kirtland Air Force Base, accessed via Wyoming Boulevard; (505) 844–8443. It's open daily 9:00 A.M.–5:00 P.M. There's no admission charge, but you must stop at the guard station at the base's entrance to obtain a museum visitor's permit. Make sure to have your current car registration and proof of car insurance, or you won't be allowed on base.

Valencia County

South of Albuquerque along I–25 you'll find the rural communities of Valencia County: Belen, Los Lunas, Bosque Farms, Jarales, and Tomé. Many of the residents of this area enjoy the rural solitude of life along the Rio Grande while benefiting from the big-city advantages of Albuquerque, only a half-hour's commute to the north.

Settled by the Spanish in 1741, Belen became a major New Mexico railroad center in the 1880s. While the railroad remains important to Belen, the heyday of passenger trains carrying travelers out West is long gone. But the **Valencia County Historical Museum** remembers. Located in the former Belen Harvey House, the small museum takes up just a part of the historic dining stop, while the rest of the restored mission-style building is occupied by the Belen Harvey House Civic Center.

In addition to displaying a variety of antique items donated by or on loan from area citizens, the museum pays homage to Fred Harvey and the days when his Harvey Houses were scattered along the railway throughout the West. Impeccable service, fine food, and the young, gracious Harvey Girls (waitresses) helped tame the wild frontier from the turn of the century until World War II, when other forms of travel took hold. One room in the museum is outfitted with furnishings typical of Harvey Girls' boarding rooms, which usually were upstairs from the dining area.

Though most of these oases of civility no longer exist, the citizens of Belen fought to save their Harvey House in the early 1980s when it faced demolition. The railroad sold the structure to the city of Belen, and residents rallied to preserve the legacy of Fred Harvey in their town.

The museum is at 104 North First Street in Belen; (505) 864–5903. Summer hours are Tuesday through Sunday from 2:00 to 4:00 P.M. (closed Monday); winter hours are Sundays from 2:00 to 4:00 P.M. and Tuesday through Thursday from 1:00 to 3:00 P.M. Hours are subject to change, so it's best to call ahead.

For a look at farm life and items from yesteryear, a visit to the **P & M Chavez Farm Museum** in nearby Jarales is a smart move. Run by Pablo and Manuela Chavez in and around their farmhouse since 1986, the museum is a wonderful mishmash of antiques and other items ranging from a late 1880s, horse-drawn hearse to a collection of 1960s Barbie dolls.

When the Chavezes were stationed in California in 1942, a fortune-teller predicted that Manuela would someday have a museum of her own. The prophecy has been fulfilled in the museum, which contains artifacts collected by the Chavezes for nearly fifty years. The museum occupies several rooms in the Chavezes house, separate from living areas, plus detached buildings, barns, and outside areas. A fine collection of antique cars—including a 1925 Studebaker, a 1959 Edsel, and a 1929 Model A Ford—and of farm implements is a highlight of the barn and outdoor exhibits. Manuela will gladly detail the background of some of the more notable displays. But don't make the mistake of asking if an item is for sale. "Nothing is for sale; this is a museum," she'll answer proudly.

From Highway 309 (Reinken Avenue) in Belen, take Highway 109 South for $3\frac{1}{2}$ miles to Jarales. The museum will be on your right; (505) 864–8354. It's open Monday through Saturday from 9:00 A.M. to 5:00 P.M. and Sunday from 1:00 to 5:00 P.M. Guided tours of the museum are $3.00 for adults, $2.00 for children, and free for kids under five. Call ahead.

If venturing to Jarales on a Friday, plan a tour of the **Valencia Flour Mill.** Not only can you see the old mill in operation, but you can also purchase freshly milled tortilla flour, whole wheat flour, wheat bran, and wheat germ.

The original mill began as the Jarales Trading Company in December 1913. The name was changed to the Jarales Roller Mill in 1919, and the mill ceased operations in the 1970s. José Cordova (grandson of the mill's founder) and his wife purchased the mill from their father's estate in 1988, and after extensive restoration the mill again began producing flour products in the summer of 1990.

The mill is located about $\frac{1}{2}$ mile from the P & M Chavez Museum (see directions above), where Jarales Road joins Mill Road; (505) 864–0305. Tours are given on Fridays from 9:00 A.M. to 4:00 P.M.; additional school tours can be arranged. No admission fee is charged.

Though the Luna-Otero Mansion was once the headquarters of a livestock and land dynasty, since 1977 the stately

Luna Mansion

home has been serving up appetizing entrees as the **Luna Mansion** restaurant. A National Historic Landmark, this is a restaurant with a story.

Domingo de Luna and Don Pedro Otero both came to New Mexico from Spain on land grants near the end of the seventeenth century. After nearly 200 years of amassing fortunes in land, livestock, and political influence, descendants of the two men's families were united by marriage in the late 1800s to create what is known as the Luna-Otero Dynasty.

The Luna-Otero Mansion was built by the Santa Fe Railroad in 1881 in exchange for right-of-way privileges through the Luna property (which meant the existing Luna home had to go). The southern colonial architectural design of the mansion is said to have been inspired by trips through the South by the Luna family. Though the design certainly seems out of place in New Mexico, the building material is not. You guessed it—it's constructed out of adobe.

Perhaps ironically, the restaurant serves up just about

everything except New Mexican food—steaks, chicken, and seafood dishes dominate the menu. The closest thing to New Mexican is the Red Chile Linguini.

The Luna Mansion is at the junction of Highways 6 and 85 in Los Lunas; (505) 865–7333. Its hours are Monday through Thursday, 5:00–10:00 P.M.; Friday and Saturday, 5:00–10:30 P.M.; and Sunday, 4:30–9:30 P.M.

Torrance County

Torrance County attaches to Bernalillo County's southeast side and is therefore a quick drive from Albuquerque. Many city residents enjoy a Sunday afternoon drive on the backside of the Sandia and Manzano mountains on Highway 337 (old South 14) and Highway 55. The atmosphere is decidedly rural and dotted with small towns along the route—Chilili (Bernalillo County), Tajique, Torreon, Manzano.

One particular bypass along the way is the **Tajique-Torreon Loop,** an incredibly scenic unpaved 17-mile stretch of road that indirectly connects the two towns. In Tajique, head east on Forest Road 55 (the road directing you to Fourth of July Campground off Highway 55). Unless you're in a four-wheel-drive vehicle, don't attempt to go past the Fourth of July Campground at the 7-mile mark—the road is clearly marked "primitive" at this point. The Manzano Mountain Wilderness, which is what the loop takes you through, is one of the few places in New Mexico where oak, maple, and aspen trees are interspersed with the usual mountain evergreens. It's a beautiful autumn drive. And if you're into camping or just want to have a picnic, the Fourth of July Campground (commonly known as Fourth of July Canyon) at the midway point is a great spot.

Old Catholic churches are the historic highlights of the towns along Highway 55 and attest to the rich Spanish traditional values of the villages. If you plan your visit during harvesttime, check out the area apple orchards. (*Manzano* means "apple" in Spanish, you know.) In recent years, the creative set has discovered some of the communities. You'll find artists, weavers, potters, and wood-carvers if you take the time to explore the area. In Torreon, along Highway 55 you'll come across two interesting businesses worth checking out: the Flower Essence Connection (505–384–5022) and Golden Earth Herb Health Products (505–384–2916). Because the owners conduct most of their business by mail order and aren't always in, call first before your trek to Torreon.

The ruins of impressive seventeenth-century mission churches and earlier pueblos are the focal points of the three units of **Salinas National Monument.** The areas included in the monument are in a basin that once held a huge lake. Because a salt marsh was left when the lake started to dry out, the Spanish explorers, upon seeing the area, named it Salinas for the salt flats. (And long before the Spanish arrived, the Indians living here used the salt as trade currency.) In the early 1600s, friars built missions at many of the pueblos in the basin. But drought, famine, and Apache raids caused both the Spaniards and the Pueblo Indians to abandon the sites by the 1670s. Over the years, the pueblos and missions were vandalized and started to collapse. It is these ruins that are now protected by the monument.

Although the ruins don't respect county lines, the monument headquarters are conveniently located between the units in Torrance County. Specifically, the visitor center is in the historic Shaffer Hotel, 1 block south of the U.S. Highway 60 and Highway 55 junction in the community of Mountainair; (505) 847–2585.

Each unit has a visitor center, picnic tables, and rest rooms, but camping is not allowed. They're all open daily 9:00 A.M.–5:00 P.M. There's no admission charge.

The most beautiful of the ruins are in the Quarai unit of the monument and are located on a well-marked road 1 mile west of the village of Punta de Agua on Highway 55. The 5-foot-thick red sandstone walls reach heights of 40 feet. Twenty-six miles south of Mountainair on Highway 55 you'll find the Gran Quivira unit. Though these are the most extensive of the ruins in the monument, because they are composed of gray limestone they are not quite so attractive as those at Quarai. The ruins at the Abó unit are similar to those at Quarai in that they are made out of red sandstone. The Abó unit is 9 miles west of Mountainair on U.S. Highway 60.

Back in Mountainair, you'll be in for a treat at **Rancho Bonito,** a space dedicated to the environmental folk art created by Clem "Pop" Shaffer during the 1930s and beyond. Since his death in 1964, Pop Shaffer's family and a dedicated corps of volunteers have restored most of the buildings to their original condition. Uniquely configured and brightly painted buildings such as "The Log Cabin" adorn the ranch. Another, "The Stone House," is completely constructed of uncut rocks accented with animal shapes. On the National Register of Historic Places, Rancho Bonito is considered a classic by folk-art organizations because of its humor and large scale.

There's no charge to visit Rancho Bonito, but it's shown by appointment only; (505) 847–2832.

Off the Beaten Path in Northeastern New Mexico

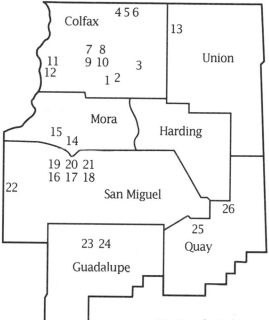

1. Santa Fe Trail Museum
2. The Livery Stable
3. Dorsey Mansion
4. Raton Historic District
5. Shuler Theatre
6. The Red Violet Inn
7. St. James Hotel
8. Old Mill Museum
9. Philmont Ranch
10. Casa del Gavilan
11. Monte Verde Ranch
    Bed and Breakfast
12. DAV Vietnam Veterans
    National Memorial
13. Capulin Volcano
14. Fort Union National
    Monument
15. La Cueva Mill
16. Rough Riders Museum
17. Plaza Hotel
18. Carriage House
    Bed & Breakfast
19. Montezuma Castle
20. Montezuma Hot Springs
21. City Pond
22. Pecos National Monument
23. Club Cafe
24. Blue Hole
25. Tucumcari Historical Museum
26. Road to Ruin

Northeastern New Mexico

The scenery of New Mexico's northeastern quadrant is quite different from that most associated with the state. Grasslands upon rolling hills and plains dominate the landscape, giving it a softer quality in comparison with the state's expansive desert regions. Some of New Mexico's oldest and largest ranches share this area with modern ski resorts.

The historic Santa Fe Trail snakes through northeastern New Mexico and figures prominently in the region's geography and history. The 900-mile trail connecting Old Franklin, Missouri, to Santa Fe was the lifeline linking the New Mexico territory to the eastern United States from 1821 to the coming of the railroad to New Mexico in 1879. Not only did the trail bring much-needed goods and prosperity; it also brought a new people, language, skills, and customs—the Anglo had come to New Mexico.

A decisive battle of the Civil War was also fought in this region on March 28, 1862, at the summit of Glorieta Pass, between Santa Fe and Pecos. In the Battle of Glorieta Pass, Union troops defeated the Confederates, thus destroying Southern hopes for taking over New Mexico.

Colfax County

The quiet community of Springer, with its tree-lined main street, Maxwell Avenue, would seem more at home in the Midwest than the plains of New Mexico. (It's the kind of town where you need to dial only four numbers to make a local phone call.) Here you'll find a slower pace, a couple of old antiques shops, and the **Santa Fe Trail Museum,** housed in the old Colfax County Courthouse, which at first glance resembles a church.

Built in 1879 when Springer sat in the county seat before Raton took over almost twenty years later, the Santa Fe Trail Museum once served as a New Mexico reform school for boys, a public library, the town hall, and the city jail before townsfolk transformed it into a museum in 1967. It commemorates Colfax County's pioneers during the time when the Santa Fe Trail was an active route crossing the region.

The museum is on Maxwell Avenue; it has no phone. It's open daily June through August; hours vary depending on the schedule of its volunteers. Admission charges are $1.50 for adults, $1.00 for seniors, and 75 cents for children.

As far as one-horse towns go, this one's got most others beat. It has its own livery stable—**The Livery Stable,** that is—which is a Springer landmark and now houses a wonderful, cluttered mishmash of antiques for sale. Hidden treasures abound. Built in 1880, the stone stable is definitely from the horse-and-wagon days and is in excellent shape, considering its age and lack of restoration. Avoid this place if a little dust and dirt offend you. The Livery Stable is at the corner of Maxwell Avenue and Third Street; (505) 483–5041. Hours vary; call ahead.

Twenty-seven miles east of Springer you'll find the grand, thirty-six-room **Dorsey Mansion.** It's pure rustic opulence in the middle of New Mexico's high plains. The log-and-stone home was built by U.S. Senator Stephen W. Dorsey of Arkansas in 1880. An addition several years later produced the castlelike structure with likenesses of the faces of Dorsey, his wife, and his brother carved in stone on the tower.

In addition to his role as a politician, Dorsey was also a railroad financier and up-and-coming cattle baron who liked to throw elaborate parties at his mansion, now listed on the National Register of Historic Places. Highlights of a tour include the black marble fireplace from Italy, the cherrywood staircase brought from Chicago, and the man-made pool with three islands, one of which once boasted a gazebo.

The mansion, currently owned by a couple from California, is protected by caretakers Ernesto and Ernestine Romero. Though it had a brief stint as a bed-and-breakfast in the late 1980s, it's now open only by appointment for tours.

To get there, take U.S. Highway 56, proceeding 24 miles east of Springer (just past the first roadside rest area) and then going north on the dirt road for 12 miles; (505) 375–2222; it's a good idea to call ahead for road conditions. There's a $5.00 charge for tours.

Just 7 miles south of the Colorado border the city of Raton evolved along the Santa Fe Trail around three main influences: coal mining, railroading, and ranching. The days of the first two are pretty much in the past. Raton's Spanish mission revival-style depot, built in 1903, served the city well until 1990, when Amtrak suspended its last scheduled stop (en route to Albuquerque from Chicago).

The depot is the focal point of the **Raton Historic District,** which centers on First Street just across from the railroad tracks. Listed on the National Register of Historic Places since 1977, the district includes some seventy buildings. Businesses originally sprang up in this area in the 1880s to serve the needs of railroad workers. Today this strip is a great place to check out antiques shops and admire the diverse architecture. You can also travel back in time at the Raton Museum, which through artifacts and photographs chronicles the area's history of mines, rails, and cattle.

The Raton Museum is located in the old Coors Building on First Street; (505) 445-8979. It's open Thursday through Saturday from 10:00 A.M. to 3:00 P.M. October through May and Tuesday through Saturday from 10:00 A.M. to 4:00 P.M. the rest of the year. There's no admission charge.

Just a block away, at 131 North Second Street (505–445–5528), the restored **Shuler Theatre** continues to stage theatrical productions. It opened in 1915 and was named for Dr. J. J. Shuler, Raton's mayor when the grand structure was built. The theater's exterior, described as European rococo architecture, pales in comparison with its interior, with its ornate woodwork, sky-painted ceiling, and gold-trimmed box seats. Eight Works Progress Administration (WPA) murals commissioned by the government during the Great Depression enhance the lobby and trace Raton's history.

The theater welcomes visitors during office hours—Monday through Friday, 9:00 A.M.–5:00 P.M.—and on weekends when a show is scheduled. There's no cost for a look or a snapshot.

As Raton's first and only bed-and-breakfast, **The Red Violet Inn** opened in the summer of 1990. Built in 1915, the imposing red-brick Victorian was purchased by innkeepers Ruth and John Hanrahan, who moved to Raton from Boulder, Colorado. Their aim to pamper is evident in the fresh-cut flowers, cookies, fruit, and sherry that await guests. The innkeepers also host a social hour for guests and townspeople daily at 6:00 P.M., when hors d'oeuvres, wine, and tea are served.

The inn's parlor flaunts "his and hers" Duncan Phyfe couches among the antique furnishings throughout the inn. The three sunny guest rooms are upstairs and share a bath that contains a claw-foot tub. Robes and sets of towels are provided for each guest.

The Red Violet Inn is located at 344 North Second Street; (505) 445–9778. Room rates range from $45 to $55.

From Raton, head 38 miles southwest on U.S. Highway 64 to discover the hidden Old West romance of Cimarron (roughly meaning "Wild" or "Unbroken" in Spanish). In fact, this *is* Marlboro Country in all its rugged, wide-open glory. Really. Those famous cigarette ads were photographed on the CS Cattle Company ranch near Cimarron. All of Old Cimarron is ripe for exploring and centered on Santa Fe Trail (that's the name of the street here; it's also *the* trail, though it becomes Highway 21 south of town).

The **St. James Hotel** in Cimarron once bedded the famous and infamous of the Wild West. Located on the Santa Fe Trail, the St. James to this day reeks of mystery and intrigue reminiscent of its past. Built in 1873 by Henri Lambert, a former cook for Ulysses S. Grant and Abraham Lincoln, the stately, pale pink adobe hotel was once considered one of the finest in the West. Jesse James, Black Jack Ketchum, Wyatt Earp, Buffalo Bill Cody, Annie Oakley, and Zane Grey were among the hotel's early patrons. The hotel was restored and reopened in 1985 by the hotel's current owners, Ed and Pat Sitzberger.

The entire hotel, including lobby, guest rooms, and dining area, is outfitted with authentic Victorian furnishings, mounted game, and large paintings. Individual rooms are now named after some of the celebrated figures who stayed in them. Evidence of the hotel's rough-and-tumble past is apparent in the bullet holes visible in the pressed-tin ceiling of Lambert's, the hotel's restaurant (previously Lambert's Saloon and Gambling Hall). Instead of red-eye, Lambert's now serves up Continental cuisine such as Shrimp Provencale and Red Rock Filet au Dijon, among pasta, beef, chicken, and veal entrees.

Every old hotel worth its salt has a resident ghost, and legend has it that the St. James was not shortchanged—no clues, though, as to who the chandelier shaker might be. For those who get caught up in the history and aura of the St. James, the hotel occasionally hosts mystery adventure weekends called "Murder on the Santa Fe Trail." Guests become actors in a staged murder they try to solve.

The St. James is on Highway 21, just north of U.S. Highway 64 in the center of Cimarron's historic district; (505) 376–2664. Room rates range from $45 to $80.

Just down the lane, across from the St. James, you'll spot the **Old Mill Museum** guarded by the thick rock walls of the Aztec Mill. The mill was built in 1864 by Lucien B. Maxwell, who, with his 1.7 million acres, was the single largest landowner in the Western Hemisphere of all time. Maxwell brought an engineer, a millwright, and a chief mason from back East to take on the $50,000 project. In its time, the mill could turn out 300 barrels of flour per day. Though the 3-story building was converted to a museum in 1967, the stone structure itself is just as impressive as its contents, which include exhibits chronicling late nineteenth-century northern New Mexico.

The museum is open daily (except Thursday) from 9:00 A.M. to 5:00 P.M. and Sunday from 1:00 to 5:00 P.M., Memorial Day through Labor Day; otherwise during May and September, it's open only on Saturday from 9:00 A.M. to 5:00 P.M. and Sunday from 1:00 to 5:00 P.M. Admission is $2.00 for adults and $1.00 for seniors, children under twelve, and scouts in uniform (read on and you'll understand). There's no phone, but the museum's curator, Buddy Morse (505–376–2913), will be glad to answer any questions.

About five miles south of the St. James on Highway 21 you'll find the headquarters to the vast **Philmont Ranch,** now owned by the Boy Scouts of America (BSA). Here's where the buffalo really do roam and the deer and the antelope are known to play. The jewel of the 137,493-acre ranch is Villa Philmonte, the Spanish Mediterranean–style mansion built as a summer home by Oklahoma oilman Waite Phillips, of Phillips 66 fame.

Phillips gave the ranch to the BSA in 1938 "for the purpose of perpetuating faith, self-reliance, integrity, freedom, principles used to build this great country by the American Pioneer." And each summer since, thousands of scouts have convened at Philmont for the ultimate camping adventure.

But nonscouts, too, can enjoy Philmont. Tours of Villa Philmonte are given daily during the summer. The home and most of its furnishings have been restored to their original grandeur. In addition to the living room, with its custom-built piano, the most impressive room is the trophy room, highlighted by the huge buffalo mounted above the fireplace.

The Philmont Museum and Seton Memorial Library (both 505–376–2281) just past the driveway that loops around the mansion are also open to visitors. The museum displays exhibits of those who influenced this area—cowboys, Indians, miners, mountain men, and settlers. The library contains the books, art, and natural history collection of Ernest Thompson Seton, an author, artist, and naturalist and the first chief scout of the BSA. The museum and library are open daily from 8:00 A.M. to 12:00 noon and from 1:00 to 5:00 P.M. June through August and Monday through Friday (same hours) the rest of the year.

Seven miles south, in Rayado, you'll find another feature of the Philmont Ranch, the Kit Carson Museum. It's built in the adobe hacienda style and finished with 1850s period furnishings. Tours are given daily June through August; call the above number for specific schedules.

If you're no Boy Scout and the St. James is booked, consider **Casa del Gavilan** ("House of the Hawk") bed-and-breakfast for a weekend hideaway. The inn was built in the early 1900s by the eastern industrialist J. J. Nairn, who often hosted famous artists and writers in his gleaming white adobe home tucked into the foothills of the Sangre de Cristo Mountains. Only those with confirmed reservations are allowed on the premises, though, because guests' privacy is highly regarded here. Casa del Gavilan is 6 miles south of Cimarron on Highway 21; (505) 376–2246. Rates range from $55 to $100 and include evening refreshments as well as breakfast.

Heading west on U.S. Highway 64 from Cimarron, you'll come across the community of Eagle Nest—along with its attractive namesake lake—and the village of Angel Fire. Between these two towns you'll find a delightfully comfortable inn, **Monte Verde** ("Green Mountain") **Ranch Bed and Breakfast.** The inn comprises most of innkeeper Sally Lebus's 1930s ranch house, which was constructed out of native granite and pine. With views of Eagle Nest Lake to the

111

north and mountains to the east, guests enjoy total comfort at Monte Verde.

Sally is certainly no uptight innkeeper. She allows guests free run of her spacious home, including a glassed-in living area with a fireplace and a huge kitchen with a wood-burning stove. Some of the guest rooms also have fireplaces, with plenty of wood available. On cool mornings an eerie mist forms over Eagle Nest Lake, adding to the setting's magic. Winter guests receive an extra: discounts on lift tickets for the nearby Angel Fire Resort ski area that Sally's family helped develop.

Monte Verde is located just off U.S. Highway 64 between mile markers 279 and 280; (505) 377–6928. Monte Verde closes to guests for about two weeks in mid-November. Rates are $45–$65; add $10 for winter rates.

The meadows meeting the mountains in the countryside surrounding Angel Fire give new meaning to the enchantment of New Mexico. Atop a small hill you'll find the country's first memorial dedicated to all Vietnam veterans. Originally built in 1971 by Dr. Victor Westphall in memory of his son, who was killed in the war, the memorial was expanded and taken over by the Disabled American Veterans in the early 1980s.

The small, nondenominational chapel at the **DAV Vietnam Veterans National Memorial** at Angel Fire is breathtakingly simple as it sits in harmony with the land. The tallest wing of this dovelike structure rises 64 feet, gracefully curving downward to the ground. The accompanying visitor center is just as contemporary and displays banners and poster-size photographs of wide-ranging scenes from the war.

Completed years before the celebrated memorial in Washington, D.C., the Angel Fire structure differs in the feeling it leaves within when visitors depart. There is no automatic turbulence or divisive political statement associated with this memorial. Though powerful in the emotions it elicits, the memorial allows visitors to come away with their own reactions, rather than forcing any particular ones.

The DAV Vietnam Veterans National Memorial is just off U.S. Highway 64 at the Angel Fire turnoff; (505) 377–6900. The visitor center is open daily 6:30 A.M.–5:30 P.M., the chapel never closes, and there's no admission charge.

Union County

What's now a perfectly cone-shaped mountain rising from the plains was once a fiery volcano that last erupted some 10,000 years ago. What's left is known as **Capulin Volcano** and is a national monument about 30 miles east of Raton. As one of the most remote and undiscovered of the nation's national monuments, Capulin rarely gets crowded.

A road from the visitor center winds 1,000 feet up the mountain to the edge of the mouth of the volcano. From here you can hike several trails. You can see four states—New Mexico (obviously), Texas, Colorado, and Oklahoma—if you hike the Crater Rim Trail. Another trail actually leads you inside the volcano—one of the few places in the world where you can do this. (Go try this in Hawaii!) Though Capulin hasn't erupted in 10,000 years, it's considered dormant, not extinct. Scientists say volcanoes 25,000 years old or less are potentially active, so no one knows if Capulin will ever erupt again. Not knowing—for certain, anyway—adds to the thrill.

To get to Capulin Volcano National Monument from Raton, take U.S. Highway 64/87 east for about 30 miles to the community of Capulin, and then head north on Highway 325 for a few miles to the monument; (505) 278–2201. The visitor center is open daily from 8:00 A.M. to 4:30 P.M. Labor Day through Memorial Day; during the summer, it's open from 8:00 A.M. to 8:00 P.M. Admission charge is $3.00 per carload, but if someone in the group is over sixty-one, everyone gets in free.

Mora County

Fort Union National Monument is at its best when visited on a crisp, sunny autumn day. Though it's quite isolated, Fort Union is easily accessible via I-25, which brings a steady stream of visitors during the summer. When approaching the remains of the fort, the vision of red-brick and adobe ruins jutting up from the grassy plains is at once both attractive and a little odd-looking. Once you get to the fort site along the Santa Fe Trail, with its incredibly expansive views, you sense why this spot was chosen.

Established in 1851 by Lieutenant Colonel Edwin V. Sumner

Ruins at Fort Union National Monument

to protect the Santa Fe Trail and the New Mexico territory from Indian raids, Fort Union was the largest military depot in the Southwest. There were actually three Fort Unions, the last of whose ruins constitute the park. The fort was abandoned in 1891, after which residents from nearby communities scavenged most of its usable materials, thereby hastening its deterioration.

The visitor center provides a walking-tour map to help interpret the fort's layout. If you visit on a sunny day, follow

114

the trail to the fort's sundial, just across from the Quarter-master's Quarters. It's still intact and quite accurate. The park service has done a great job preserving the frontier feeling and dignity of the fort. Interpretive audio stations at selected stops along the trails emit dialogues indicative of the situation, that is, soldier to commander, soldier to soldier. And recorded bugle calls sporadically echo across the grounds from loudspeakers hidden by the adobe walls. Fort Union is also one of the best places to see the wagon-wheel ruts of the Santa Fe Trail, those wagons last cutting through the plains more than a century ago.

To get to Fort Union, take I–25 north of Las Vegas to Exit 366, and then head north on Highway 161, which dead-ends at the fort after 8 miles; (505) 425–8025. A tree-shaded picnic area is available. The park is open daily 8:00 A.M.–5:00 P.M. The admission price is $1.00 per person or $3.00 per carload.

Just outside the community of Mora, you'll encounter **La Cueva Mill,** a beautifully rustic old structure now part of Mora County's Salman Ranch. The mill was built by Vicente Romero in the 1870s, partly in response to the heavy demand for flour owing to the establishment of Fort Union and to the steadily increasing Santa Fe Trail traffic. Though Mora County is now one of New Mexico's most economically depressed areas, during the late 1800s it was one of the most prosperous.

The old adobe and stone buildings of the mill are not accessible, for safety reasons; nevertheless, you can pull off the road for an exterior look at one of New Mexico's more impressive old water-driven mills. The cold, clear water from the acequia (man-made ditch) still flows around the mill, though it's now diverted from the wheel.

While the mill has not been used for grinding wheat and generating electricity since 1949, during late summer through early fall Salman Ranch sets up shop at the mill to sell its produce, including vegetables, herbs, cut flowers, and, most notably, farm-fresh raspberries. You can also stock up on the ranch's prized raspberry jam. And its raspberry vinegar is perfect for dressing a salad.

The mill is located 6 miles south of Mora near the junction of Highway 518 and Highway 442. In-season produce sale hours are generally 9:00 A.M.–5:00 P.M., Tuesday through Sunday. For more information, call the ranch at (505) 387–2742.

San Miguel County

Often confused with the glitzier and much-younger gambling capital of Nevada, the community of Las Vegas, New Mexico, has a charm all its own. During its railroad heyday in the 1880s, Las Vegas ("The Plains") was the largest and most exciting city in New Mexico. Today, Las Vegas has mellowed into a captivating community enhanced by a rich architectural heritage—half the state's registered historic buildings, more than 900, are located here.

To get a sense of Las Vegas's past, stop by the **Rough Riders Museum.** If you're fortunate, you'll visit on a day when Harold Thatcher is on hand. As curator for the past twenty years, Mr. Thatcher will fill you in on the history of the museum and the stories behind the exhibits.

The museum is named for the heroic group of men Teddy Roosevelt organized for his acclaimed Cuban campaign during the Spanish-American War. Many of the volunteers came from New Mexico, and the Rough Riders later held a reunion in Las Vegas every year from 1899 (when the event was attended by Roosevelt while he was governor of New York) until 1967, when it was attended by only one veteran, Jesse Langdon, who later died in 1975. In Las Vegas, Roosevelt even announced his candidacy for president and twice stayed at the Plaza Hotel (see below).

The museum began with mementos brought home by the Rough Riders and now includes a great variety of artifacts relating to Las Vegas's history and New Mexico's past. The museum is located at 727 Grand Avenue; (505) 425–8726. It's open Monday through Saturday 9:00 A.M.–4:00 P.M. There's no admission charge.

Many native New Mexicans consider Las Vegas's Old Town Plaza the most beautiful plaza in the state because of its largeness, abundance of trees, and gazebo. Anchored by the historic **Plaza Hotel,** the streets around and adjacent to the plaza are dotted with shops and restaurants.

One hundred years after it originally opened, and following a $2 million renovation, the Plaza Hotel reopened in 1982 to its former Victorian grandeur. From the worn hardwood of the lobby floor to the towering twin staircases connecting the lobby to the second floor, the Plaza Hotel has an air of

Plaza Hotel

history and elegance. Except for the modern comforts of queen-size beds and new bathrooms, the high-ceilinged guest rooms are appointed in period antiques with wall and window treatments consistent with the Victorian era. As a welcome change from many historic hotels, the guest rooms are surprisingly well insulated and are thus quiet, each offering its own thermostat.

Byron T's, the lobby bar, is named after former Plaza Hotel owner Byron T. Mills, who's also the hotel's resident ghost. It's a comfortable place to enjoy a drink while having a street-level view of the plaza. The hotel's restaurant, the Landmark Grill, features New Mexican dishes as well as beef, fish, and chicken entrees. Pasta specialties like Tortellini Primavera and Seafood Linguini Alfredo round out the menu.

The hotel is located at 230 on the Old Town Plaza; (505) 425-3591. Room rates range from $47 to $77.

For a more intimate overnight adventure in Las Vegas, consider a stay at the **Carriage House Bed & Breakfast.** The inn is housed in a 3-story Queen Anne–style mansion built in 1893, one of the many architectural gems found throughout Las Vegas's inner core of historic districts. As Las Vegas's only bed and breakfast, the Carriage House doubles as an antiques shop, offering up most of the inn's period furnishings as well as additional selections. The Carriage House is located at 925 Sixth Street; (505) 454–1784. Room rates range from $34 to $39.

Head out of Las Vegas about 6 miles on Hot Springs Road (which borders the streetside corner of the Plaza Hotel) and you'll be in the small community of Montezuma at the mouth of Gallinas Canyon. The imposing **Montezuma Castle** looms on a hilltop as the focal point for Armand Hammer United World College of the American West. Built in 1884 as a show-piece resort by the Santa Fe Railroad, Montezuma Castle was abandoned as a hotel during the financial depression at the turn of the century. The castle was purchased in 1981 by the late Dr. Armand Hammer—billionaire philanthropist and for-mer chairman of Occidental Petroleum Corporation—with the intent of starting the college. The small college now has more than 200 students from more than sixty nations. Although the castle itself is not regularly open for tours, you can get a closer view by driving or walking around the campus.

Just past the castle on Hot Springs Road (Highway 65) are the **Montezuma Hot Springs,** nondescript holes that dot the banks of the Gallinas River. Located on the property of the United World College, these natural hot tubs are fed from mineral springs that bubble up from the ground. The springs are a great place to relax and enjoy the view—Montezuma Castle, the river, the rock cliffs—especially when it's a little nippy outside. A brown sign, HOT SPRINGS BATHS, marks the spot. There's no charge to enjoy the therapeutic waters, but it's a first come, first soak arrangement. Early morning and late night are the best times to find them vacant. You may encounter naked people milling about, so if this offends you, consider yourself warned.

About ½ mile farther on Highway 65 toward the mountains, veer left on a gravel road and you'll immediately come across **City Pond.** During most times of the year the pond is nothing more than a small body of water bordered by shimmering, sheer cliffs on one side. But during the dead of winter, when the water has frozen and the ice skates have been brought out, the pond turns into a winter wonderland reminiscent of the Northeast and Midwest. It's one of only a few places open to the public in New Mexico where you can pond-skate.

Heading south from Las Vegas, plan a stop at **Pecos National Monument,** near the community of Pecos. The park boasts one of the most attractive visitor centers (Spanish hacienda-style, with impressive woodwork) and the friendliest park rangers in the state. The monument preserves the ruins of the abandoned Cicuye Pueblo. Before you start exploring, be sure to view the short film—narrated by actress Greer Garson, a former New Mexican resident—which dramatically presents the history of the pueblo site. The film will put you in the right frame of mind to better appreciate what you'll see later. It's screened every twenty minutes or so.

The park includes a walking tour, as well as a museum containing artifacts relating to the Indians, the Spanish, and the Anglo pioneers who lived at or affected the monument site. While exploring the trails that wind among the ruins, you can climb down a ladder into a restored kiva (ceremonial chamber) and see the *sipapu*, the small hole in the ground believed to connect to the spirit world in the center of the earth. To see evidence of the Spanish colonial influence, you can walk through the remains of a missionary church. The scenery is inspiring as it varies from plains, mesas, and mountains in the distance.

To get to the monument from Las Vegas, take I–25 south to the Pecos exit and proceed on Highway 63; (505) 757–6414. It's open daily 8:00 A.M.–5:00 P.M. The admission charge is $1.00 per person or $3.00 per carload.

Guadalupe County

The **Club Cafe** in Santa Rosa is one of those few remaining classic Route 66 eateries. You know the type: lots of neon, friendly folks, great food, and just the right touch of tacky. It's owned by Santa Rosa writer Ron Chavez and hasn't changed much since its 1935 opening. The cafe and its

The Road to Ruin is located on U.S. Highway 54 in Logan; (505) 487–2444. It's open daily from 10:00 A.M. until whenever people leave (2:00 A.M. max.).

Off the Beaten Path in Southeastern New Mexico

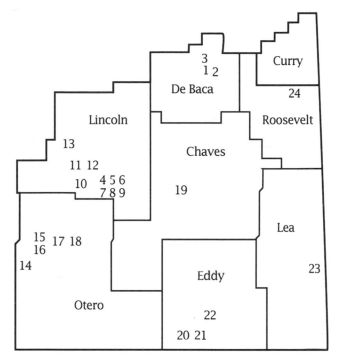

1. Old Fort Sumner Cemetery
2. Fort Sumner State Monument
3. Billy the Kid Museum
4. Lincoln State Monument
5. Casa de Patrón
6. Wortley Hotel
7. San Patricio
8. Fort Meigs Galleries
9. Tinnie Silver Dollar
10. Sierra Mesa Lodge
11. Smokey Bear Museum
12. Chango's Restaurant and Art Gallery
13. White Oaks
14. White Sands National Monument
15. Eagle Ranch Pistachio Groves
16. Space Center
17. Cloudcroft
18. The Lodge
19. Roswell Art Center and Museum
20. Carlsbad Caverns National Park
21. New Cave
22. Living Desert State Park
23. Lea County Cowboy Hall of Fame and Western Heritage Center
24. Blackwater Draw Museum

Southeastern New Mexico

Probably the most diverse region of the state, southeastern New Mexico can't be pigeonholed. Its varying landscape ranges from the harshness of the high desert and the glistening dunes of White Sands to the cool peaks of the Sacramento Mountains and the evergreen-laden Lincoln National Forest. Fertile river basins like the Hondo Valley produce pastoral scenes of horses grazing on green fields of oats, as well as vistas of orchards teaming with crisp, red apples. And vast areas of rich, irrigated cropland help feed the nation, thanks in part to the legendary Pecos River (as in "west of the Pecos").

De Baca County

De Baca County *is* Fort Sumner and Fort Sumner *is* Billy the Kid. Without a doubt, the Kid is New Mexico's most famous legend who actually lived. Though only twenty-one when he died, William Bonney, also known as Billy the Kid, created a legacy and a legend that just won't die. And the community of Fort Sumner is one of several locales in New Mexico where the Kid left his mark. It's also where his remains remain.

In the **Old Fort Sumner Cemetery,** you can visit the grave of Billy the Kid. Graves are few and scattered in the small military cemetery, but the most prominent site is encaged in metal—a three-person grave, Billy's alongside those of two of his pals, Tom O'Folliard and Charlie Bowdre.

The Kid's tombstone has a history of its own. It was first stolen in 1950, and its whereabouts remained a mystery until 1976, when Joe Bowlin, owner of the Old Fort Sumner Museum adjacent to the cemetery, recovered it in Granbury, Texas. Several years later it was again stolen, but this time it was recovered within days, in California. The Kid's tombstone, now shackled in iron for protection, has an epitaph that reads THE BOY BANDIT KING/HE DIED AS HE HAD LIVED.

Each summer during the second weekend in June, Fort Sumner hosts Old Fort Days. Here a favorite event is, appropriately enough, the World's Richest Tombstone Race, wherein participants run while carrying a replica of Billy's tombstone.

To get to the cemetery (which is just behind the Old Fort Sumner Museum), head east on U.S. Highway 60/84 from Fort Sumner for 3 miles and then take a right onto Billy the Kid Road (Highway 272), proceeding for 4 miles. There's no admission charge to enter the cemetery, and it's always open.

The Old Fort Sumner Museum (505–355–2942), in front of the Old Fort Sumner Cemetery, contains artifacts from Fort Sumner's past. Historical paintings line the walls, while Billy the Kid newspaper clippings and photos are posted on easels throughout. If you have time on your hands, you can learn a lot about the Kid by reading the news items. Otherwise, check out the barbed-wire collection and the old Apache moccasins and articles of Indian ceremonial dress. The museum also has items that were purchased from the La Paloma Museum when it closed down in Lincoln several years ago.

Old Fort Sumner Museum is open daily from 8:00 A.M. to 6:00 P.M. during the summer (roughly Memorial Day through Labor Day) and from 9:00 A.M. to 5:00 P.M. the rest of the year (although it may close early if business is slow), with the exception of January through March when it closes for the winter. Admission is $2.00 for adults, $1.00 for children under thirteen, and free for those under six.

About ¼ mile down the gravel road in front of the museum you'll find **Fort Sumner State Monument** (505–355–2573). It's here where the town gets its name, because the monument's grounds include the ruins of the old military fort. A small visitor center tells the story of Fort Sumner and showcases items excavated from the fort. Late autumn is a great time to visit, for instead of seeing other people you'll get to take a gander at the migratory birds making patterns in the blue sky above nearby Bosque Redondo, the 16 miles of wooded wetlands along the Pecos River.

Fort Sumner was created because of a horrible experiment that failed. During the Civil War, settlers in New Mexico and Arizona, feeling they were in constant danger from the non-Pueblo Indians living in the territory, built the fort as part of a new reservation on which to relocate the Mescalero Apaches and the Navajos. For five years 9,000 Indians were confined to the reservation, after having been forced to walk hundreds of miles from their homelands. Because disease and shortages of food and firewood plagued the reservation, General William T. Sherman sent the Indians home in 1868. At the monument you'll see a shrine dedicated in 1971: a small pile of rocks carried from different parts of the Navajo Nation in northwestern New Mexico and northeastern Arizona to commemorate "The Long Walk."

The fort site is also where Billy the Kid was gunned down by Lincoln County Sheriff Pat Garrett on July 14, 1881, years after the 1869 abandonment of the fort.

The monument is open Thursday through Monday, 9:00 A.M.–6:00 P.M. Admission charge is $1.00, with children under sixteen admitted free.

Back in the modern-day community of Fort Sumner, you'll come across the most fun of this off-the-beaten-track area's unique spots. If you're a true lover of the legend, you might just satiate your hunger for Kid artifacts and lore at the **Billy the Kid Museum.** The privately owned facility was opened as a one-building museum in 1953 and now rambles both indoors and out through several structures.

You can spend several enjoyable hours strolling among the more than 60,000 relics—some historic, some pure kitsch—collected over the years by Ed Sweet, former owner of the museum, and his wife, Jewel. This place just plain smells old, a wonderfully sentimental scent, as if hundreds of grandmothers' houses were combined.

Kid artifacts include his guns, a jail-cell door that imprisoned the outlaw, and even locks of his hair saved by a Las Cruces barber. There's also an original Billy the Kid "wanted" placard signed by territorial New Mexico governor Lew Wallace (author of the novel *Ben Hur*). In addition, you can view a fine selection of antique cars (some of which are usually parked out front, for effect), as well as fossilized dinosaur droppings.

The museum is located at 1601 East Sumner Avenue, 2 miles east of downtown; (505) 355–2380. It's open daily from 8:30 A.M. to 5:00 P.M. May 15 to September 15 and on Monday through Saturday (same hours) the remainder of the year, with the exception of January and February, when the museum closes. Admission is $2.00 for adults, $1.00 for children under twelve, and free for those under six.

Lincoln County

No other town in New Mexico has preserved its past more meticulously than the community of Lincoln, nestled in the Bonito Valley. History buffs of the Southwest will want to spend the whole day in Lincoln because the entire town is a National Historic Landmark, thus making visible commercialism absent. As Bob Hart of the Lincoln County Heritage Trust notes, "You will find no rubber tomahawks here." Much of the one-street town constitutes the **Lincoln State Monument** and other museums.

As with many old, remote New Mexico towns, Lincoln has definitely seen its wilder days. The former county seat achieved its notoriety as the site of one of the Wild West's bloodiest events: the Lincoln County War of 1878. The war was the culmination of a dispute between opposing factions vying for political and economic control—especially of the city's lucrative mercantile business, which included nearby Fort Stanton. Billy the Kid got his infamous start during the conflict, in which he sided with one of the factions. Eventually he became a fugitive and, much later, after being captured, made his daring escape from the Lincoln County Courthouse in 1881—only to be tracked down in Fort Sumner by Sheriff Pat Garrett (see De Baca County entry). The 2-story courthouse is part of the Lincoln State Monument. It's said that Billy's gun is responsible for a bullet hole visible in the wall at the foot of the stairwell.

A single ticket, available at the Lincoln County Historical Center along U.S Highway 380, provides access to all the historical sites in town. Though everything is open daily from 9:00 a.m to 6:00 P.M. May through September, hours and accessibility vary during other times of the year. Tickets are $4.50 for those over fifteen, and children are admitted free. Call (505) 653–4025 for more information.

The most distinctive lodging in the area can be found at **Casa de Patrón,** a bed-and-breakfast along Lincoln's main street. The primary part of the inn was built in the mid-1800s as the home of Juan Patrón, the youngest speaker of the house in New Mexico's territorial legislature. A gracious host, Patrón entertained the likes of pre-outlaw Billy the Kid and territorial governor Lew Wallace in his home. Today, the

old adobe home continues to delight those who find themselves in this isolated part of New Mexico.

Hosts Jeremy and Cleis Jordan escaped the stress—and
humidity—of Houston in the early 1980s to settle into the
laid-back—and dry—landscape of Lincoln. Jeremy, an engi-
neering consultant, and Cleis, a classical musician, occasionally treat their guests to "salon evenings" based on a particular theme, such as "An Evening in Vienna," in which an
elegant dinner is combined with a concert performed by
Cleis on the inn's grand piano.

For those who want to enjoy a longer stay or have a place
to themselves, the Jordans offer two cabins as part of their
inn: Casita Bonita and Casita Paz ("Small Pretty House" and
"Small Peace House," respectively). The inn's grounds are the
most handsome patch of green in Lincoln—a comforting contrast for the eyes.

Casa de Patrón is on U.S. Highway 380; (505) 653–4676. An
ever-changing breakfast, complete with freshly ground coffee, is included in the daily rate of $45–$90.

The **Wortley Hotel** is another fine place to stay in Lincoln,
and it's the only public place to get a meal for miles. The
original structure was built in 1874 but burned to the ground
in the 1930s. The current replica was constructed some
thirty years later and is owned by the Museum of New Mexico system. The small, comfortable rooms are simply done in
period furnishings reflecting Lincoln's heyday in the late
1800s. For a great diversion on a lazy Lincoln afternoon, settle into one of the many old rockers on the porch spanning
the Wortley's facade and close your eyes as the creak-creak
lulls you back to Lincoln's colorful past.

The Wortley is situated along U.S. Highway 380 in Lincoln;
(505) 653–4500. It's open May through September, and rates
range from $32 to $49. Its restaurant serves three meals
daily during the season.

In the placid Hondo Valley east of the resort town of Ruidoso (known for Ruidoso Downs, home of the world's richest
quarterhorse race, and as the place where well-heeled Texans
summer amid galleries and boutiques), you'll find one of the
most tranquil, unaffected spots in southern New Mexico: the
tiny community of **San Patricio,** along the Rio Ruidoso.

This is a place of horse ranches and apple orchards. It's

Wortley Hotel porch

also a thriving arts community—a well-hidden fact because of its low-profile location. It's neither promoted nor pretentious. San Patricio is where some of the surviving members of the Wyeth-Hurd creative dynasty continue to paint. Though the family tree has many branches of artists, some of the most celebrated members include N. C. Wyeth, Andrew Wyeth, Peter Hurd, and Henriette Wyeth.

The most imposing and beautiful brick structure in San Patricio houses the very polished La Rinconada Gallery (505–653–4331). Built by Mike Hurd, the gallery features the art of members of the Wyeth-Hurd family, including that by Peter Hurd and Henriette Wyeth.

But the most absolutely and incredibly fascinating spot to visit for any die-hard art adventurer is across the road: **Fort Meigs Galleries.** Am I gushing yet? There truly aren't enough superlatives to describe this peculiar place or the man behind it. John Meigs is one of the last true renaissance men. Encouraged to come to New Mexico almost four decades ago by the late Peter Hurd to assist in painting murals, Meigs's life reads like an adventure novel: He sailed to Tahiti on the eve of Pearl Harbor's attack (and again a few years ago); he was the designer of the original "Hawaiian shirt" (collector's items now, not modern rip-offs synonymous with tackiness); and he's a veteran of both the San Francisco and the New York art scenes, as well as an international jet-setter extraordinaire.

A close friend of Georgia O'Keeffe and the Wyeth-Hurd clan, Meigs collected their art as well as art and assorted artifacts the world over. Now it's all for sale in his rambling home/galleries located on this prime patch of pastoral San Patricio. Meigs even goes so far as to say, "Everything's for sale, even me. Just make an offer."

You'll find antique architectural fixtures and Samoan tapestries sharing space with the likes of a soldier's trunk (dated discharge papers lining the inside) from George Washington's army. But the art takes center stage in the many Mexican-tiled and whitewashed rooms of the galleries—filled with the works of both famous and obscure talents.

Call ahead to make sure John will be there when you arrive (he has others staffing the galleries when he's away, though), and set aside a few hours to savor the art and the accompanying stories. Fort Meigs Galleries are in San Patricio just off (south) of U.S. Highway 70. Take the gravel road to the left around the old church and the polo field (yes, the polo field) and follow the signs; (505) 653–4320. It's open daily 9:00 A.M.– 5:00 P.M.

Farther east on U.S. Highway 70 you'll come across the tiny town of Tinnie. The focus here is the **Tinnie Silver Dollar**— restaurant, bar, old-time mercantile, and gallery. The red-roofed adobe structure with its wooden bell tower dominates the landscape and provides a wonderful time-travel experience inside.

Alternately a private residence, mercantile company, and post office dating from 1882, the building became a restaurant in 1959 and was later reconditioned to become the polished gem of southeastern New Mexico. The Silver Dollar's authentic Brunswick bar in its lounge and the hand-beveled glass, fine art, and exquisite antiques galore provide a visual feast for diners. Especially notable is the Victorian Room, which hosts special one-sitting dinners featuring a custom predetermined menu. Selections from the regular menu include a full range of steaks and seafood, most notably Tinnie's Choice-Cut Ribeye and Pasta Diablé (shrimp sautéed with tomatoes, basil pesto, crushed red pepper, and white wine, served atop green chile fettucini).

During the summer the Silver Dollar hosts jazz festivals and serves drinks on its long veranda. The colorful and carefully landscaped backyard that slopes toward the Rio Hondo adds to this establishment's charm—and its appeal as a site for weddings.

In addition to the high-society glamour of territorial New Mexico it provides for its ordinary customers, the Silver Dollar is also patronized by some of New Mexico's most powerful economic and political players who like to keep a low public profile.

Adjacent to the restaurant and bar you'll find a mercantile/ gallery that sells everything from flour to Arabian horses, including a selection of locally made gifts. The manager explains that the store stocks things for community residents, not tourists, adding, "If we don't have it, you don't need it."

The Silver Dollar is on U.S. Highway 70 near the intersection of Highway 368; (505) 653–4425. Dinner hours are 5:00–10:30 P.M., Wednesday through Sunday. Lunch is served Saturday and Sunday 11:30 A.M.–4:00 P.M.

If you like the unusual but are weary of the old and historic, check out **Sierra Mesa Lodge** outside the small town of Alto. It's a squeaky clean and comfortable bed-and-breakfast inn tucked into the Lincoln National Forest. Each room is furnished in a theme ranging from Victorian or Queen Anne to French country or country western. Whichever you select, be assured you'll get a large room, a queen-size bed, and a private bath.

Sierra Mesa is the most luxurious lodging closest to Ski Apache, located on Sierra Blanca, southern New Mexico's highest peak. In addition to the skiing at Ski Apache, winter is a perfect time to visit the inn because of its glass-enclosed hot-tub room that looks out into the snowy forest. Sierra Mesa's hot-tub policy of "one couple at a time" adds to the romance of this place. Also, such added extras as "tea and pastry" afternoons and "wine and cheese" evenings in front of the fireplace can't be beat.

Sierra Mesa Lodge is 2 miles east of Alto on Fort Stanton Road; (505) 336–4515. Rooms go for $85 per night, including breakfast for two.

The favorite son of the village of Capitan wasn't even human. He was none other than Smokey Bear. (No one knows where that pesky middle name "the" came from, but for the record it's *not* Smokey *the* Bear.) Yes, it's a fact, the national symbol of forest-fire prevention really did exist, and he lived right here in the Capitan Mountains. And the now-legendary story of Smokey's life is amazingly accurate.

In May 1950, a fire crew rescued a badly singed bear cub that had been clinging to a charred pine tree after devastating fires destroyed much of the Lincoln National Forest near Capitan. After recuperating at a veterinary hospital in Santa Fe, Smokey was flown to the National Zoo in Washington, D.C., where he "spoke out" for forest-fire prevention until his death in 1976. He was buried in Capitan in the Smokey Bear Historical State Park.

Adjacent to the park you'll find the **Smokey Bear Museum,** which documents Smokey's story. The museum contains several scrapbooks filled with photographs and news clippings on Smokey's life and times. The fact that a museum would even make scrapbooks accessible to visitors is odd, but the effect is very personal, down-home, and nostalgic—a detail that adds to the melancholy feeling of this small log museum.

There's a bigger-than-life-size upright Smokey that speaks at the press of a button—the perfect replica to get your picture taken with. An exhibit of Smokey Bear toys, books, and comics from the 1950s and 1960s shows how popular culture was used to convey an important message to the youth of the era.

The museum is on First Street in downtown Capitan; (505) 354–4290. It's open daily from 9:00 A.M. to 5:00 P.M. May to September and on Friday through Tuesday from 10:00 A.M. to 4:00 P.M. the rest of the year. There's no admission charge.

For an international flavor deep in the heart of Lincoln County, check out **Chango's Restaurant and Art Gallery.** Opened in 1982 by chef/artist Jerrold Flores, Chango's is a favorite of area innkeepers. While it may seem out of place in the small community of Capitan, the food is definitely uptown in both presentation and flavor. Entree selections change weekly on Jerrold's whim but also in reflecting the cuisines of different countries. Recent selections have included Poached Salmon in Piñon Sauce, and Orange Roughy with Pistachios and Asparagus.

The gallery part of Chango's, which is primarily the restaurant walls, features contemporary art and antiques, collectibles, and primitive art. Like the food, the art also changes regularly. As an avid art collector, Jerrold often highlights items from his personal holdings. Recent exhibits include masks from East India, Mexico, and Guatemala; Japanese kimonos; and Imperial Chinese items.

Chango's is at the corner of First Street and Lincoln Avenue; (505) 354–4213. It's open Thursday through Saturday from 5:00 to 9:00 P.M.

Farther north in Lincoln County you'll find the remains of New Mexico's most raucous mining town in the ghost town of **White Oaks.** One version of White Oaks's birth in the 1870s says that the discoverer of the North Homestake mine sold it to a friend for $40, a pony, and a bottle of whiskey. He probably lived to regret that decision when the mine eventually produced $500,000 in gold.

Along came other mines with names like Rip Van Winkle,

White Oaks Bar and Museum

Large Hopes, Little Hell, and Smuggler, and the boomtown was under way, with a population that swelled to 4,000. The town became a hangout for cattle rustlers and outlaws, including Billy the Kid. Saloons, gambling houses, and "houses of another sort" took hold as White Oaks entrepreneurs thought of quick ways to wheedle away the day's take from area miners.

White Oaks faded when a planned railroad link with El Paso went instead to the New Mexico town of Capitan. Besides, the gold played out at about the same time.

A simple historical marker, a cemetery, and many abandoned buildings are all that's left of old White Oaks. A few hardy folks have rediscovered the town, elevating its status to semi-ghost town. An impressive building is Hoyle's Castle, a brick Victorian mansion that looms over the town from its hilltop site. A retired schoolteacher from Carrizozo lives in the structure, which resembles a classic haunted house out of an old movie. It's not open to visitors.

White Oaks does have a bar and a museum. They're one and the same, housed in the old post office, a tiny wooden shack near the center of town. It's not only an interesting place in which to look at relics from the mining days but also a fun, though eerie, place in which to grab a beer and play a game of pool in the back room.

White Oaks is 9 miles off U.S. Highway 54 on Highway 349, 11 miles northeast of Carrizozo.

Otero County

Driving into Otero County from the north along U.S. Highway 54, observant motorists and spider fanciers should be on the lookout for the brave tarantulas that cross the highway on warm summer days. I'm sure highway department TARANTULA CROSSING signs wouldn't last out here, as less-than-honest souvenir-seekers would pick them off as fast as they could be placed. Tarantulas aside, Otero County offers weekend adventurers several special spots. Though much of the county is off-limits (White Sands Missile Range, Fort Bliss Military Reservation, and the Mescalero Apache Indian Reservation), the parts that are accessible make up for it.

The missile range isn't the only place that's privy to the soft, snow-white gypsum dunes just southwest of the city of Alamogordo. Adjacent to the range is the **White Sands National Monument**—part of the largest gypsum dune field in the world—whose majesty you're welcome to explore.

This extremely stark park is the perfect place for uninhibited barefoot frolicking. It's also the place for people who are afraid of the water: lots of beach, no ocean. Pack plastic sleds and snowboards to slide down the up-to-60-foot-tall sand dunes. During the height of summer, the sand tends to get quite hot, but you wouldn't want to visit then anyway—tourists, you know. Plan a late autumn visit—or, better yet, camp out during a full moon (allowed at a backcountry campsite only; registration required). At night, the reflection of moonlight from the sand provides an unearthly adventure you won't soon forget—it's bright enough for reading!

A visitor center/museum explains how the dunes were formed and contains an exhibit on those species of plants and wildlife hardy enough to thrive in such a harsh environment. Still, it's the Dunes Drive, an 8-mile scenic loop, that forms the highlight of a visit to White Sands. The "sands" are almost like a living entity. Gusting winds cause them to shift, which makes keeping the roads clear a full-time chore. Occasionally, the Dunes Drive is closed because of missile-range testing, so call ahead.

White Sands National Monument is 15 miles southwest of Alamogordo, just off U.S. Highway 70/82; (505) 479–6124. It's open daily, with hours as follows: in summer (Memorial Day through Labor Day), visitor center 8:00 A.M.–7:00 P.M. and Dunes Drive 7:00 A.M.–10:00 P.M.; in winter, visitor center 8:00 A.M.–4:30 P.M. and Dunes Drive 7:00 A.M. to sunset. There's a $3.00 fee per private vehicle for the Dunes Drive; it's $1.00 per individual for bus groups, hikers, and cyclists.

Just north of Alamogordo you'll find **Eagle Ranch Pistachio Groves,** producer of "Heart of the Desert" pistachio nuts. Though the bulk of domestic pistachio farming occurs in the fertile San Joaquin Valley in California, a new agricultural industry has emerged in this southern New Mexico town after a little research showed that climate and elevation factors were nearly perfect in Alamogordo for growing the fickle nut.

Never dyed red to appeal to consumers or cover blemishes, Eagle Ranch's off-white and green nuts are available only by mail or at the ranch store. The outlet recently introduced red chile pistachios for die-hard New Mexican chileheads who need an extra kick to everything they eat.

Marianne Schweers, who owns the groves with her husband, George, shares an interesting bit of pistachio lore: When the Shah of Iran was overthrown in 1979, not only was the world oil market affected but the Middle Eastern country's other principal export also suffered when its markets were cut off. Yes, until that time Iran was the world's premier pistachio supplier. The situation was a big boost to U.S. pistachio production, and the timing couldn't have been better for fledgling Eagle Ranch. Marianne sums up the situation by saying, "The Ayatollah was the best friend that [U.S.] pistachio growers ever had."

Though visitors are always welcome to look at the groves, guided tours are available only to groups of ten or more. The Eagle Ranch store, which also sells other southwestern food and gift items, is located 4 miles north of Alamogordo on U.S. Highway 54/70; (505) 434–0035. The store is open daily 9:00 A.M.–6:00 P.M.

In Alamogordo ("Fat Cottonwood"), you'll find the **Space Center** nestled in the foothills of the Sacramento Mountains. This shimmering, massive gold cube of a building houses four levels of museumlike exhibits in the International Space Hall of Fame (annual induction ceremony held the last Saturday in September).

You start on the top floor and work your way down ramps through exhibits like the "There's Space in New Mexico" room, which combines traditional New Mexico ambience— adobe walls, pine-planked floor, vigas (wood ceiling beams)— with the state's cutting-edge research and contributions to the nation's space program. You can also step inside the interactive Space Station 2001 exhibit for an astronaut's view of space travel in the future, as well as examine a Skylab space suit and even Soviet space food.

For those who want to take a load off, the Space Center is also home to an Omnimax theater with a 2,700-square-foot screen, as well as to a high-tech planetarium system. Outside, on the grounds of the Space Center you'll find the John P. Stapp Air and Space Park, which is filled with actual space hardware and rocket equipment. This is also a good place to get a broad view of White Sands in the distance.

To get to the Space Center, turn east on Indian Wells Road off U.S. Highway 54/70/82 in Alamogordo and follow the signs; (505) 437–2840. It's open daily 9:00 A.M.–6:00 P.M. Hall of Fame admission charges are $2.25 for adults and $1.75 for children ages six to twelve; theater admission charges are $3.75 for adults and $2.50 for children; and kids under six are admitted to both attractions free. There are also special combination rates and family, senior citizen, and active-duty military rates. (*Note:* Admission for all attendees is free to the Hall of Fame on the day of the annual induction ceremony; see above.)

Highway 82, from Alamogordo to the village of **Cloud-croft,** is one of southern New Mexico's most beautiful drives. In just 16 miles you'll climb nearly 5,000 feet, passing through all the climatic zones from the Sonoran Desert region of Mexico to the Hudson Bay region of Canada. As the road winds through the forested Sacramento Mountains, you'll come across many scenic overlooks, as well as roadside stands selling apples, cider, and various other forms of produce. New Mexico's only highway tunnel is also on this route.

Once you experience the breathtaking setting of Cloudcroft high in the Sacramentos, you'll understand why getting here is worth the effort. The small town is a year-round playground where you can beat the heat in the summer and marvel at the turning of the aspens in the fall. And Cloudcroft's magical winters bring snow skiing at Cloudcroft Ski Area, the southernmost ski area in the United States, and ice skating at Sewell Skate Pond, one of only a few outdoor places in the state where you can pursue this sport.

Cloudcroft is also home to **The Lodge,** a romantic mountain getaway. This place has a history. Built as a railroad resort in 1899, the inn was reconstructed after the original lodge burned in 1909. Famous guests include Judy Garland and Clark Gable, and Conrad Hilton, founder of the hotel chain that bears his name, owned the place in the 1930s.

The Lodge's European-style architecture, with its 4-story copper tower, adds to a mood of romantic seclusion in a chalet high in the Alps. Inside, Victorian ambience takes over in the high-ceilinged guest rooms outfitted with antique furnishings and down comforters. Select a stay when your weary bones need a rest and you couldn't care less about roaming the byways for further adventure.

Because it's usually chilly at this altitude (9,200 feet), expect a cozy fire in the lobby fireplace any time of year. Just off the lobby is Rebecca's, the lodge's dining room, named after the ghost who is said to roam the inn's halls; Rebecca, the story goes, was a flirtatious, redheaded chambermaid who in the 1930s was killed by a jealous lover. For a more casual atmosphere, check out the Red Dog Saloon in the lodge's basement.

The Lodge is just off Highway 82 in Cloudcroft; (505) 682–2566. Room rates range from $55 to $150, depending on the particular room and season.

Chaves County

The city of Roswell is one of those near-perfect all-American cities. Cited by national publications as one of the ten best small cities in the country, Roswell has also been included in the list of "Ten Peaceable Places to Retire" compiled by *Money* magazine. As the largest city in southeastern New Mexico, Roswell has its share of interesting sites and cultural diversions as well as the century-old New Mexico Military Institute. But the most impressive spot to visit is the **Roswell Art Center and Museum.** With twelve galleries in the grand adobe structure, the center focuses on art, history, and science.

Known for its excellent paintings of the Southwest, the center has the finest single collection of art in southeastern New Mexico. Featured New Mexico artists include Georgia O'Keeffe, Ernest Blumenschein, Henriette Wyeth, Andrew Dasburg, and Fremont Ellis. The museum's nationally acclaimed Hurd Collection is the most extensive collection of Roswell-native Peter Hurd's works.

A special wing of the center displays the actual engines and rocket assemblies developed by Dr. Robert H. Goddard, who worked in Roswell from 1930 to 1942. The Goddard Wing also has a replica of the early space scientist's laboratory, where he built the world's first liquid-fuel rockets.

The museum is located at 100 West Eleventh Street; (505) 624–6744. It's open Monday through Saturday from 9:00 A.M. to 5:00 P.M. and Sunday from 1:00 to 5:00 P.M. There's no admission charge.

Eddy County

Eddy County should probably be called Cave County. In addition to containing the world-famous Carlsbad Cavern, the county has untold numbers of other caves, most of them patiently waiting to be discovered by some daring young spelunker. And if the name were changed to Cave County, the county seat would undoubtedly be **Carlsbad Caverns National Park,** probably the single most visited spot in New Mexico and certainly one of the best known.

Despite its name, the park is located not in Carlsbad but, rather, 26 miles southwest of the city. Actually, it's closer to Whites City, named after Jim White, who discovered this underground fantasyland in 1901. Because you'll be underground in a constant-temperature (read: quite-cool) environment during most of your visit, pleasant weather is not a major factor for enjoyment. Therefore, it's a good idea to avoid the crowds of summer, when the above-ground temperatures can soar.

From May through October the park offers visitors the fun of viewing mass bat flights. After dusk, almost a million Mexican freetail bats swirl out of the cave's entrance for their nightly escapades and insect-feeding frenzies. The bat flight is preceded by informative—and humorous—talks by rangers about the tiny winged mammals. Though it's true that these same bats are in the cave during the day, don't worry: The caverns are enormous, and you won't even notice the slumbering bats.

Though the park is decidedly remote, access is no problem. Of course, after making the significant trek to the park you'll undoubtedly want to view the famed stalactites and stalagmites decorating the grand chambers of Carlsbad Cavern, but as a true adventurer you'll more likely be drawn to **New Cave.**

New Cave preserves some of the thrill cavers experience when exploring a new find. The two-hour, guided lantern tour (limited to groups of twenty-five) takes you through the undeveloped cave in all its eerie, dark splendor. You'll need to bring along a flashlight, water, and nonslip shoes. (*Note:* Don't attempt a New Cave adventure unless you're in reasonably good physical shape.) In a remote section of the park is the world's largest cave: Lechuguilla Cave, whose magnitude was discovered only in 1986. It's designated a "wild" cave and open just to experienced cavers in organized expeditions (park permit required). Neither does the National Park Service plan to develop Lechuguilla; it, along with several other wild caves, may be designated the world's first cave wilderness.

The park entrance is located just west of Whites City on Highway 7. Because there are various phone numbers at the park, call the Carlsbad Chamber of Commerce at (505)

887–6516 for specific information. Though Carlsbad Cavern is open daily with continuous self-guided tours, New Cave features only two tours daily during the summer (Memorial Day through Labor Day) and on weekends the rest of the year. Reservations are recommended. Tour charges for New Cave are $5.00 for adults and $3.00 for children under sixteen. (*Note:* This tour is not recommended for small children.)

Closer to the city of Carlsbad you'll find **Living Desert State Park.** This unique park atop the Ocotillo Hills combines botanical gardens and a zoo in a natural setting. It concentrates on plants and animals indigenous to the Chihuanhuan Desert. You'll see mountain lions, bobcats, buffalo, antelope, and the endangered Mexican wolf, as well as an excellent collection of exotic cacti and succulents from around the world. The views of Carlsbad and the Pecos River Valley from parts of the trail are spectacular.

The park is located just off Highway 285 on Skyline Drive in the northwest edge of Carlsbad; (505) 887–5516. It's open daily from 8:00 A.M. to 8:00 P.M. (last tour at 7:00 P.M.) May 15 through Labor Day and from 9:00 A.M. to 5:00 P.M. (last tour at 4:00 P.M.) the rest of the year. Admission is $3.00 per person, with children under six admitted free.

Lea County

The Llano Estacado, or "Staked Plains," makes up a large part of the landscape of New Mexico's southeasternmost county, one of the last major land areas in the continental United States to be settled. Homesteading and open-range ranching were a way of life on this often-harsh land during the early part of this century. For the most part, working cowboys have given way to rodeo cowboys in these parts. In fact, Lea County has produced more professional rodeo champions than any other county in the United States, starting with Henry Clay McGonagill in 1901. He was the first professional rodeo cowboy. In 1978, the county's heritage was honored with the founding of the **Lea County Cowboy Hall of Fame and Western Heritage Center** in the county's largest city, Hobbs.

The result of the dream of Dale "Tuffy" Cooper, the Hall of Fame captures the essence of the early days and the pioneers of Lea County. It honors county residents who have distinguished themselves in rodeo, as ranch cowboys, or as pioneer or present-day women on ranches. In contrast to many museums, the chronologically displayed exhibits are glimpses of history depicting entire scenes rather than just labeled artifacts. Complete portrayals of a pioneer bedroom and kitchen look as though someone might return any minute. Memorabilia of all inductees are also displayed in the Hall of Fame.

The Hall of Fame is on the campus of New Mexico Junior College, 5317 Lovington Highway, in Hobbs; (505) 392–4510, ext. 371. It's open Monday through Friday, 8:00 A.M.–5:00 P.M.; Saturday, 9:00 A.M.–5:00 P.M.; and Sunday, 1:00–5:00 P.M. There's no admission charge.

Roosevelt County

North of the city of Portales—the home of Eastern New Mexico University—you'll come across one of the most significant archaeological sites in North America: Blackwater Draw. And the **Blackwater Draw Museum** is on hand to help interpret exactly why this spot is so important. (The Blackwater Draw site is actually a little northwest of the museum, but visit the museum first.)

On this site in 1932, A. W. Anderson of nearby Clovis discovered the oldest evidence of man's existence in the New World—11,000 years ago. Spear points, bones, and fossilized remains of woolly mammoth, saber-toothed tiger, camel, and bison have been recovered from the sprawling maze of canyons. At one time Blackwater Draw was a large pond used as a watering hole for animals and, subsequently, as an ambush site for the early human inhabitants. The pond dried up 7,000 years ago, eventually forcing the hunter-gatherers to move on.

While the museum displays some of what has been discovered at the site, archaeological excavations continue. Over the years, the digs have been funded by the likes of the Carnegie Institute, the National Geographic Society, and the Smithsonian Institution.

The museum is located 7 miles northeast of Portales on

U.S. Highway 70; (505) 562–2202. From Memorial Day through Labor Day, the museum is open Monday through Saturday from 10:00 A.M. to 5:00 P.M. and Sunday from 12:00 noon to 5:00 P.M.; during other times of the year, hours remain the same except that the museum is closed on Monday. The site's hours are the same during the summer; however, it's closed December through February and is open only on weekends (museum hours) during the spring and fall seasons when it will also close during inclement weather. Admission is $2.00 for adults, $1.00 for seniors and children (ages six to fifteen), and free for children under six. (A single ticket allows visits to both museum and site.)

Appendices

New Mexico Indian Pueblos
(Keyed to county where most of the reservation is located)

Bernalillo County

Isleta
P.O. Box 317
Isleta, N.M. 87022
(505) 869–3111

Cibola County

Acoma
P.O. Box 309
Acomita, N.M. 87034
(505) 242–1139

Laguna
P.O. Box 194
Laguna Pueblo, N.M. 87026
(505) 552–6654

McKinley County

Zuni
P.O. Box 339
Zuni, N.M. 87327
(505) 782–4481

Rio Arriba County

San Juan
P.O. Box 1099
San Juan, N.M. 87566
(505) 852–4400

Santa Clara
P.O. Box 580
Española, N.M. 87532
(505)753–7326

Sandoval County

Cochiti
P.O. Box 70
Cochiti, N.M. 87041
(505) 465–2244

Jemez
P.O. Box 78
Jemez, N.M. 87024
(505) 834–7359

Sandia
P.O. Box 6008
Bernalillo, N.M. 87004
(505) 867–3317

San Felipe
P.O. Box A
San Felipe, N.M. 87001
(505) 867–3381

Santa Ana
Star Route, Box 37
Bernalillo, N.M. 87004
(505) 867–3301

Santo Domingo
Box 99
Santo Domingo, N.M. 87052
(505) 465–2214

Zia
General Delivery
San Ysidro, N.M. 87053
(505) 867–3304

Santa Fe County

Nambé
Route 1, Box 117–BB
Santa Fe, N.M. 87501
(505) 455–7692

Pojoaque
Route 11, Box 71
Santa Fe, N.M. 87501
(505) 455–2278

San Ildefonso
Route 5, Box 315–A
Santa Fe, N.M. 87501
(505) 455–2273

Tesuque
Route 11, Box 1
Santa Fe, N.M. 87501
(505) 983–2667

Taos County

Picuris
P.O. Box 127
Penasco, N.M. 87553
(505) 587–2519

Taos
P.O. Box 1846
Taos Pueblo, N.M. 87571
(505) 758–9593

Non–Pueblo Indian Reservations in New Mexico
(Keyed to the county where most of the reservation is located)

Navajo Nation
Tourism Division
Window Rock, Ariz. 86515
(602) 871–7545
(San Juan and McKinley counties in New Mexico but also in northeast Arizona and southeast Utah)

Other Locations of Navajo Chapters in New Mexico:

Alamo Chapter
Alamo Route
Magdalena, N.M. 87825
(505) 854–2267
(Socorro County)

Cañoncito Chapter
P.O. Box 398
Laguna, N.M. 87026
(505) 831–3957
(Bernalillo County)

Ramah Chapter
P.O. Box 308
Ramah, N.M. 87321
(505) 783–5901
(Cibola County)

Jicarilla Apache Reservation
P.O. Box 507
Dulce, N.M. 87528
(505) 759–3242
(Rio Arriba County)

Mescalero Apache
  Reservation
P.O. Box 176
Mescalero, N.M. 88340
(505) 671–4495
(Otero County)

New Mexico Wineries

Alamosa Cellers
P.O. Box 690
Elephant Butte, N.M. 87935
(505) 744–5319

Anderson Valley Vineyards
4920 Rio Grand Boulevard NW
Albuquerque, N.M. 87107
(505) 344–7266

Balagna Winery
(San Ysidro Vineyards)
223 Rio Bravo Drive
Los Alamos, N.M. 87544
(505) 672–3678

Binns Winery
3910 West Picacho
Las Cruces, N.M. 88005
(505) 526–6738

Blue Teal Tasting Room
P.O. Box 1263
Mesilla, N.M. 88046
(505) 524–0390

Devalmont Winery
(Gruet Méthode Champenoise)
3758 Hawkins NE
Albuquerque, N.M. 87109
(505) 344–4453

Domaine Cheurlin Winery
(Méthode Champenoise)
P.O. Box 506
Truth or Consequences, N.M.
 87905
(505) 744–5418

La Chiripada Winery
Box 191
Dixon, N.M. 87525
(505) 579–4437

La Viña Winery
P.O. Box 121
Chamberino, N.M. 88027
(505) 882–2092

Las Nutrias Winery
P.O. Box 1156
Corrales, N.M. 87048
(505) 897–7863

Madison Winery
Star Route 490
Ribera, N.M. 87560
(505) 421–8028

Mountain Vista Vineyards
1325 Foothill Road SW
Albuquerque, N.M. 87105
(505) 877–4345

St. Clair Winery
P.O. Box 112
Deming, N.M. 88031
(505) 546–9324

Sandia Shadows Winery
11704 Coronado NE
Albuquerque, N.M. 87122
(505) 298–8826

Santa Fe Winery
203 Calle Petaca
Santa Fe, N.M. 87505
(505) 753–8100

Tularosa Vineyards
Star Route 2, Box 5011
Tularosa, N.M. 88352
(505) 585–2260

Index

Index

Index

Index